Gregor Mendel

And the Roots of Genetics

Owen Gingerich
General Editor

Gregor Mendel

And the Roots of Genetics

Edward Edelson

Oxford University Press
New York • Oxford

Oxford University Press

Oxford   New York
Athens   Auckland   Bangkok   Bogotá   Buenos Aires   Calcutta
Cape Town   Chennai   Dar es Salaam   Delhi   Florence   Hong Kong   Istanbul
Karachi   Kuala Lumpur   Madrid   Melbourne   Mexico City   Mumbai
Nairobi   Paris   São Paulo   Singapore   Taipei   Tokyo   Toronto   Warsaw

and associated companies in

Berlin   Ibadan

Design: Design Oasis
Layout: Leonard Levitsky
Picture research: Lisa Kirchner

Library of Congress Cataloging-in-Publication Data

Edelson, Edward
Gregor Mendel / Edward Edelson.
p. cm. — (Oxford Portraits in Science)
Includes bibliographical references and index.
Summary: Explores the life of Gregor Mendel, an Austrian monk whose
experiments with pea plants became a foundation for modern genetics.
ISBN 0-19-512226-7 (hardcover); 0-19-515020-1 (paperback)
1. Mendel, Gregor, 1822–1884—Juvenile literature. 2. Geneticists—Austria—Biography—Juvenile literature. [1. Mendel, Gregor, 1822–1884. 2. Geneticists.]
I. Title. II. Series.
QH31.M45E34   1999
576.5'092—dc21   98-37541
[b]   CIP
                               AC

9 8 7 6 5 4 3 2

Printed in the United States of America
on acid-free paper

On the cover: Gregor Mendel in the days of his experiments; Inset: Mendel as Abbot.

Frontispiece: Medal commemorating the 100th anniversary of Mendel's papers on heredity.

Contents

OXFORD PORTRAITS IN SCIENCE

Members of the Augustianian monastery in Brno in the early 1860s. Gregor Mendel is standing at the far right, holding a fuchsia bloom.

Mendel is Discovered

In January 1884, the local newspaper in the city of Brno (then called Brünn and in the Austro-Hungarian Empire, today in the Czech Republic) noted the death of the beloved abbot of the Brno monastery. The obituary said that the abbot, Gregor Mendel, was an enthusiastic scientific researcher, spending many hours on studies in meteorology and beekeeping, and growing different kinds of flowers, "especially a full and beautiful fuchsia." It also briefly mentioned "his observations of plant hybrids, which he grew in large numbers." A hybrid is a new kind of plant created by crossing two distinctly different species or varieties of plants.

A quarter of a century later, in 1910, thousands of people gathered in the square outside the monastery to honor Gregor Mendel. The crowd included a number of renowned scientists, from every country in Europe. A statue commemorating Mendel was unveiled, and the square was renamed in his honor.

Mendel was being honored for the work with plant hybrids that had not seemed very important during his life. One speaker, a German scientist named Erich Tschermak, said that Mendel's experiments in which he crossed plants with different characteristics had made inheritance "a rational, indeed mathematical, problem" and that Mendel had created "an exact method of research into heredity." Others praised Mendel as the father of a new science, genetics. The basic rules of that science had been established by Mendel's work with plant hybrids, and the field already was being called Mendelian genetics.

What had happened between Mendel's death in 1884 and the 1910 celebration was the discovery, or rediscovery, of the findings resulting from the scientific studies of plant inheritance that Mendel had conducted as far back as the 1860s. At the turn of the 20th century, several scientists who were ready to report their new findings on inheritance did a routine search of the scientific literature and found that Mendel had made the same discoveries more than three decades earlier. Mendel had not been secretive about it. He had published his results in a scientific journal and sent 40 copies of his paper to scientists and institutions. They were ignored. The scientific world was simply not ready to appreciate Mendel's approach to inheritance, an approach based on mathematical analysis of the traits that are passed from generation to generation. Other scientists working in the general field of inheritance did not use mathematics to describe their results, so they did not appreciate the importance of his results. That appreciation came decades later when other scientists doing the same kind of experiments began to apply mathematical analysis to their work. Then they could look at Mendel's results with new eyes and give him the credit he deserved.

But another reason why Mendel's achievements were not immediately recognized was that he did not publish additional reports in multiple scientific journals or advise more scientists of his results. We do not know why Mendel did not make this extra effort. Maybe his responsibilities as abbot of his monastery or the illness that developed in his

text continues on page 13

HEREDITY BEFORE MENDEL

The mystery of heredity puzzled scientists for many centuries before Mendel did his work, and a number of theories were proposed to explain why one individual was like its mother, another like its father, and still another like a grandparent.

Aristotle, in a 19th-century engraving.

One of the first theories was proposed in the fifth century before Christ in Greece by Hippocrates, who is considered to be the founder of medical science. His theory, called pangenesis, said that minute particles from every part of the body entered the seminal substances of the parents, from which the new individual was formed, and so that individual exhibited the traits of both parents.

A century later, Aristotle proposed a different theory that said every part of the new organism was contained in the father's semen, which shaped the new individual by acting on the menstrual fluid of the mother. Aristotle was the first to say that the mother played an essential role in heredity.

In the third century A.D., St. Augustine wrote that God had endowed matter with certain powers of self-development, a proposal that left open the question of natural causes in the production of plants and animals.

The next round of theory-making did not occur until the 17th century. In Holland, Antoni van Leeuwenhoek, using the newly developed microscope, said that he was able to see a tiny, fully formed embryo in a woman's womb that developed into a new individual

continued on page 12

(continued from page 11)

when it came in contact with the sperm. That observation was the basis of the theory of preformation.

But in the next century, the French scientist René-Antoine de Réaumur proposed that there were organic molecules in the seminal substances of both parents, and that when they fused, a special force acted on them to produce the new individual. This theory, called epigenesis, was developed in many ways by a number of scientists over the next decades. Many scientists assumed that the organisms created at the start of the universe had simply replaced themselves endlessly over the following generations. That idea was abandoned when examination of fossil remains in the eighteenth century revealed forms of plants and animals that no longer existed.

Work by 18th-century scientists such as J. G. Koelreuter on the creation of hybrid plants reopened the question of how new individuals were created. Koelreuter returned to Aristotle's theory, saying that the seminal substances of both parents played a role. Koelreuter became a supporter of the theory of epigenesis, contradicting the still-popular belief in preformation.

The argument between proponents of the two theories went on for decades and included speculation on evolution. The great 18th-century French biologist George Buffon stressed the influence of environment on heredity, an idea that was picked up and amplified by Jean-Baptiste de Lamarck. Charles Darwin's theory of evolution explained that the offspring of parents could have many different traits, and that natural selection determined which of those traits were passed on to become the basis of new species.

But Darwin and all the other scientists concerned with heredity had no explanation for the way that traits were passed from generation to generation. So when Mendel began his work on plant hybrids, he was seeking to answer what was perhaps the oldest question in biology.

text continued from page 10

later years and eventually killed him had something to do with it, but those are just guesses.

Or perhaps Mendel simply felt that he had done enough. One of his fellow monks, Franz Barina, recorded some of Mendel's last words: "Although I have had to live through many bitter moments in my life, I must admit with gratitude that the beautiful and the good prevailed. My scientific work brought me much satisfaction, and I am sure it will soon be recognized by the whole world."

The basic principles that Mendel described are still the foundation stones of the science of genetics. It is a science that is having an enormous impact on our lives, not only in such endeavors as cloning and genetic engineering but also in the practice of medicine. A modest man working in a quiet corner of Europe had opened the door to the 20th-century science of genetics without being noticed.

Who was Gregor Mendel? The world began to ask that question after his rediscovery. A complete answer was not available. Many of his private papers had been burned by the man who succeeded him as abbot, because they were regarded as worthless. And Mendel was not a demonstrative man. The quiet life of the monastery in which he spent most of his years suited him. As one historian of science said, "Mendel's was a sober mind. His thoughts were mainly concerned with concrete facts, and he had little inclination for sentimentalism of any sort."

But Mendel was noteworthy enough in Brno for much of what he did to be recorded during his lifetime, and many persons who knew him were still alive in the 20th century to give their reminiscences. Much of his correspondence with other scientists had been preserved. Every now and then, a previously unnoticed paper or letter

A medal commemorating the 100th anniversary of the donation of Mendel's papers to the Brno Natural History Society in 1865. The banner shows the ratio of dominant and recessive alleles resulting from Mendel's hybrid pea experiments.

by or about Gregor Mendel came to light, a process that continues to this day.

What also continued for many decades after his death was scientific and political controversy about Mendel's findings. Some scientists could not accept his principles, and some political movements had their own reasons for objecting. The Communists of the Soviet Union, for example, believed they could breed a new kind of man and woman, free from the constraints of conventional Mendelian genetics. One pseudoscientist, Trofim Lysenko, loudly proclaimed in the 1940s and 1950s that Communism had disproved Mendel, and that traits created by the beneficial rule of Communism already were changing the next generation, because they were being passed to newborn children in spite of Mendel's rules of inheritance. Lysenko won the support of Joseph Stalin, the ruthless Soviet dictator, and Mendel's rules were officially outlawed in the Soviet Union and the Eastern European countries that it controlled at that time. Under Communism, the Mendel Museum in his monastery was closed. Scientists were able to save the documents and instruments dating from Mendel's time only at the last minute.

The vicious Nazism of Germany in the 1930s and 1940s was also hostile to Mendel's findings. An article published during the German occupation of Czechoslovakia in World War II falsely described Mendel as someone who thoroughly rejected Darwin's theory of evolution. That attitude changed decisively after Germany's defeat in 1945.

Lysenkoism lost favor after the death of Stalin in 1959 and died out before the end of the Soviet Union in the 1990s. The Mendel Museum was reopened and material relating to him and his research were collected once more. And when a meeting was held in Brno in 1965 to celebrate the 100th anniversary of Mendel's historic paper, a representative of Russia was there to pay tribute. B. L. Astaurov, president of the All-Union Society of Geneticists and

Selectionists, a Russian organization, said in a speech, "The real penetration into the very essence of the phenomena discovered by Mendel required such a radical change of biological thinking as can be compared to the transition from the Newtonian mechanics to the ideas of modern quantum physics."

Mendel's work has survived and research based on it has flourished in every free country. And the story of Gregor Mendel, man and scientist, remains an inspiration to many young scientists.

Because of the time gap between his death and his rediscovery, the full story of Gregor Mendel may never be known. But the documents that survived and the people who remembered Mendel have given a picture of Mendel the scientist and Mendel the man, a picture that will pass on to future generations.

MENDEL AND COMMUNISM

I n February 1948, the Communist Party took power in Czechoslovakia, which was then under the control of Moscow. In August of that year, a conference on the state of the biological sciences took place in Moscow, under the control of Trofim Lysenko. At the opening session of the conference, Lysenko declared genetics to be a false bourgeois science, which he referred to in scathing terms as Mendelism. That science, Lysenko said, was to be replaced by a new biology based on the principle that characteristics of one generation could be passed on to the next generation regardless of Mendel's principles. Lysenko's idea was that the Soviet state would produce a new and better human being in just a few years—something that Mendel's laws said was impossible.

The Mendel monument, which was transferred to the garden of the Brno monastery in 1962.

In September 1950, the golden jubilee of the rediscovery of Mendel's principles was celebrated at Ohio State University. Geneticists and other scientists from all over the world attended—but none from the Soviet Union and countries that it controlled. A few months earlier, Czechoslovakian secret police had closed the Augustinian monastery in Brno and arrested its monks. The monastery buildings were made into factories, and the greenhouse that Mendel had used in his experiments was destroyed. In 1959, a Communist official ordered Mendel's statue removed from the square that had been named for him; it was sent to the yard of the factory that had once been the monastery.

Supporters of Mendel removed documents from the Mendel Museum and saved them in trunks in the nearby Moravian Museum. For some reason, the Communists did not change the name of Mendel Square.

Everything began to change after the death of Joseph Stalin, the Soviet dictator. The most effective criticism of Lysenko was made by a geneticist who was released from a labor camp in Siberia, Nicolai Timoleev-Ressovsky, and by another geneticist, Josef Krizenecky, who said that for Lysenko to deny the Mendelian conception was like rejecting the law of gravity. Krizenecky was arrested after he made that statement and was imprisoned for 18 months. But he continued his efforts on behalf of Mendel.

In 1962, he was given the job of establishing a Mendel museum in Brno and of preparing for a celebration of the centenary of Mendel's publications, but he died before he could get very far.

In August 1965, however, a Gregor Mendel Memorial Symposium was held in Brno under the auspices of the Czechoslovak Academy of Sciences, the International Union of Biological Sciences, and a number of other international organizations. That meeting heard a statement by H. J. Muller, a Nobel Prize winner for his work in genetics, who said that the brilliant work of Gregor Mendel contains the main clue to the means by which life arose out of nonliving material.

Also in 1965, the Mendel Museum was reestablished in the building where Mendel had done his work. The Mendel Museum has since been host to scientists from many countries. And in 1990, the monks in the Order of St. Augustine were allowed to return to the monastery where Mendel had spent most of his life. The monastery is now trying to establish an institute for the study of Mendel's legacy to modern genetics.

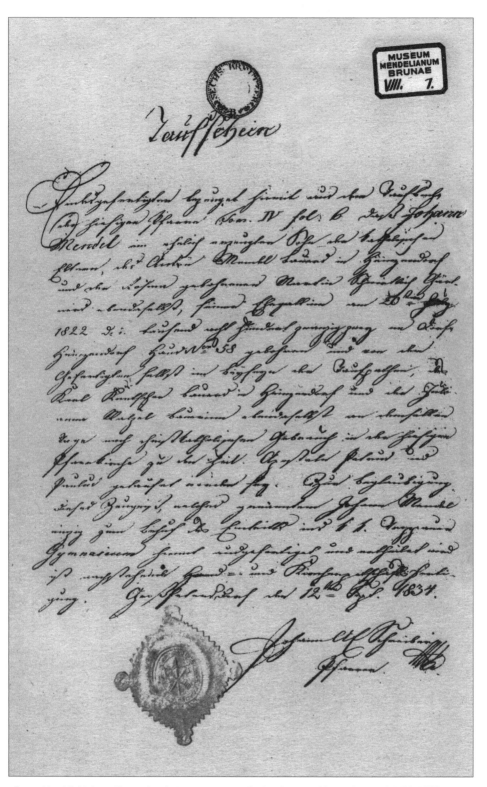

Gregor Mendel's birth certificate—handwritten, as was standard at that time. He was born on July 22, 1822.

Young Mendel Chooses the Monastic Life

On July 22, 1822, Anton Mendel, a farmer in the village of Hyncice in the province of Silesia, part of the Hapsburg Empire, recorded the birth of a son to his wife, Rosine. They named the boy Johann. (Johann changed his name to Gregor in later years.) Johann Mendel grew up as an only son. A girl, Veronica, had been born two years before him. Another girl, Theresa, was born seven years after him. There were other siblings, but they all died at birth.

Anton Mendel had been a soldier during the Napoleonic Wars, serving in the Austrian army. At the time of his son's birth, he farmed a small plot of land, with a garden where he grew fruit trees and had beehives. The Mendels were not dirt-poor. Anton had enough money to rebuild his wooden house in brick, and he owned two horses. (The main features of the house and farmstead are still preserved, and the two rooms of the living quarters house a memorial exhibition to Gregor Mendel.)

Gregor Mendel's two sisters—Veronica on the right, Theresa on the left—with Theresa's husband, Leopold Schindler, in the middle.

But money was never plentiful in the Mendel house. According to the feudal customs that still were maintained in the early 19th century, Anton had to work three days a week for his landlord, half of that time supplying a team of horses. There was plenty of work for young Johann Mendel to do on the farm, from the earliest time that he was able to work.

Young Johann was not destined to be a farmer like his father, largely because he was lucky with regard to his place of birth. There was a village school in Hyncice; many other towns in that country had no school at all. The village was part of the estates of Countess Walpurga Truchsess-Zeil, who had a strong interest in educating the children living on her estates. Young Johann began to attend the village school as soon as he was old enough. One of the principles by which the school was run was "money and property can be taken from me, but never the art of scientific knowledge." Among other things, Johann Mendel and the other pupils in the school gathered thousands of fruit tree seeds, which produced seedlings that were grown to improve the stock.

The teachers soon noticed that young Mendel was an unusually intelligent boy, and in 1833, they arranged for him to attend a more advanced school in Lipnik, some 25 kilometers—about 16 miles—from Hyncice. Johann did well at the new school, and the next year, he was transferred to the more advanced *Gymnasium* (roughly the equivalent of an American high school), as such a school was called, in Opava, 36 kilometers from home.

Sending Johann to *Gymnasium* was not an easy decision for his parents to make. They were still paying off a loan they had taken to build their house, and they had to scrape and save to pay his tuition. They also had to give up the idea of having their son take over the farm when his father grew older. But young Mendel did go to *Gymnasium,* and his parents sent him bread and other foods from their farm whenever they could. Johann came home only briefly, during the school holidays. He helped to support himself at school. Because he was an excellent student, he was able to give lessons to his schoolmates for a fee.

The Mendels did not have good luck with their harvests in the next few years, because of bad weather, and their money soon ran out. Young Mendel made a very practical decision: He would study to be a teacher so that he could earn money by being a tutor even while he continued his education.

In an autobiography that he submitted 15 years later as part of a job application, Mendel, writing of himself in the third person, said, "Owing to several successive disasters, his parents were completely unable to meet the expenses necessary to continue his studies, and it thereby happened that the respectfully undersigned, only 16 years old, was in the sad position of having to provide for himself entirely. For this reason he attended the course for school candidates and private teachers at the district teachers' seminary in Opava. Since, following his examination, he was highly recommended in the qualification report, he succeeded by private tutoring during the time of his humanity studies in earning a scanty livelihood."

The school in Opava had a natural history museum, which had been set up in 1814 and was improved continuously through the years. One of the subjects it covered was meteorology, in which Mendel had a lifelong interest. Studies at the *Gymnasium* lasted for six years. Graduates who wanted to attend a university had to undergo another two years of what was called philosophical study, which covered the history of philosophy as well as mathematics and was taught either by an institute attached to a university or by a

Gregor Mendel attended the secondary school at Opava from 1834 to 1840.

separate Philosophical Institute. The nearest such institute for Mendel was in the city of Olomouc.

A fragment of poetry that young Mendel wrote while at the *Gymnasium* has survived. In it, Mendel pays tribute to the power of the written word and expresses the opinion that scientific knowledge would rid the world of superstition. He also mentions that he would like to contribute to the growth of scientific knowledge.

Mendel graduated from the *Gymnasium* in 1840, when he was 18. He wanted to continue his education but ran into bad financial luck. No one wanted his private tutoring, so he could not earn the money he needed for school. He became very ill, for the first of several times in his life. The details are unclear, but it appears that he suffered what we today would call a nervous breakdown, one that was so severe he spent the next year at home with his parents.

As Mendel described it in his own words, "When he graduated from the *Gymnasium* in the year 1840, his first care was to secure for himself the necessary means for the continuation of his studies. Because of this, he made repeated attempts in Olomouc to offer his services as a private tutor, but all his efforts remained unsuccessful because of a lack of friends and references. Sorrow over these disappointed hopes and the anxious, sad outlook which the future offered him affected him so powerfully at that time that he fell sick and was compelled to spend a year with his parents to recover."

His father had suffered a serious physical injury while farming and asked him to take over the farm, but young Mendel still wanted to continue his education. In 1841, he enrolled in the Philosophy Institute in Olomouc; he would have to study there for two years before he could be admitted to the university. He still had difficulty making a living, and he became ill again during examination time for the first term—but he managed to finish with high grades in mathematics and Latin philosophy. After recuperating at home for some time, he returned to the Institute in Olomouc and completed his studies there over the next two years.

Meanwhile, Mendel's older sister Veronica married, and she and her husband took over the farm. The contract of sale provided that young Mendel would be given 100 gold florins and an additional 100 florins a year while he was in school, but only if he eventually became a priest or should he in any other way begin to earn an independent livelihood. (They also offered free room and board if he could not support himself in any way.) The condition about becoming a priest was to prove significant a few years later. The younger sister, Theresa, helped Johann by offering him part of her dowry, the money that had been set aside for her marriage. Mendel was so grateful that many years later he supported Theresa's three sons in their college studies.

Another significant fact was that Mendel took a course in physics at the university, in addition to his studies in philosophy, ethics, and mathematics. The course was taught by a professor named Friedrich Franz, who was a member of a Catholic order of priests. The meeting of Franz and Mendel was significant in two ways. The longer-term significance was that the study of physics accustomed Mendel to a mathematical approach to the world in general and to studies of plants in particular, something that would take decades to make itself felt. More immediately, the contact with Franz played a role in perhaps the most significant decision in Mendel's life.

As Mendel described it later in his third-person autobiography, the effort to earn a living was becoming more and more intense. "It was impossible for him to endure such exertion any further," Mendel wrote of himself. "Therefore, having finished his philosophical studies, he felt himself compelled to enter a station in life that would free him from the bitter struggle for existence. He requested and received in the year 1843 admission to the Augustinian monastery of St. Thomas in Brno."

F. C. Napp, abbot of the Augustinian monastery in Brno from 1824 to 1868, was an early mentor for Mendel. He encouraged Mendel to pursue the study of natural science.

There were many other applicants for admission to the monastery. The Augustinian abbot in Brno, F. C. Napp, had asked Franz to keep an eye open for likely candidates. Franz recommended only one, Mendel, who, he said, had "during the two-year course in philosophy almost invariably had the most exceptional reports" and was "a young man of very solid character, in my own branch almost the best." Franz added that although Mendel spoke Czech poorly, he was ready to work on it. The ability to speak Czech was important because that was the main language at the monastery;

Mendel had grown up in a family that spoke German, the other major language in the area. Because of Franz's recommendation, Mendel was admitted without even taking the interview that was standard for most applicants.

Mendel entered the monastery as a novice (a person admitted as a probationary member) at the age of 21, on September 7, 1843. When he did, as was the custom, he adopted a new name: Gregor, the name by which we now know him.

Today many people think that a man who becomes a monk and enters a monastery is cutting himself off from the main currents of the world. Mendel's experience was quite different. To start with, he no longer had to struggle to provide himself with the bare necessities of life. After he took care of his priestly duties, he had ample time for study. And his priestly duties were limited: he became so upset and ill when he visited sick patients at a nearby hospital to offer them religious consolation that F. C. Napp, the abbot of the monastery, relieved him of that duty and others. For the first year, following the orders of his superiors, Mendel studied classical subjects. After that, he was able to spend most of his time in the study of natural science, about which he wrote that he had a special liking, which deepened the more he had the opportunity to become familiar with it.

And the Brno monastery, like many others, was a center of intellectual life that made the study of natural sciences relatively easy. The monastery, well endowed by gifts of money and property from local families, had a large library. Because the monastery was a major property owner, its abbot had a seat in the diet (congress) of the province, which gave it added influence. When it was founded in the 14th century, the monastery was located in the center of the city of Brno. It was famous for having the then famous Black Madonna painting, an image of the Virgin Mary that, legend said, had been painted by the Apostle Luke and was reputed to have supernatural powers. During the 17th century, the monastery

was expanded to provide accommodations for 42 monks, and a large library was established. But in the 18th century, it experienced an upheaval caused by the hostility of Emperor Josef II (1780–90) to the Church. Many monasteries were abolished. The one in Brno was not, but the monks had to leave their centrally located building and move to quarters on the outskirts of the city. The building was dilapidated, and the cost of renovating it left the community of monks in debt. Nevertheless, the monks were active in the intellectual life of their city and country. Over time, the monastery's

The former Queen's Monastery in Old Brno became the seat of the Augustinian Order in 1873. This image is from the period when Mendel lived in the monastery.

power and influence increased. The head of the monastery was given the title of abbot, which was rarely done at that time. Prominent families frequently bequeathed land to the monastery, which steadily increased its wealth.

Each of the monks had well-furnished quarters, usually a two-room apartment. The day started early at the monastery. The monks arose at 6 A.M. for morning mass and prayers. Many went to do parish work or teach. Those who did not could study in the library; if it did not have a book they needed, they could order it from a nearby or distant bookstore or publisher. Mendel studied theology and philosophy, which were mandatory even after the probationary period, and chose natural science as an elective subject. His study of theology began after a year of probation. During that year, he attended lectures on agricultural science, which were compulsory, and also lectures at the Brno Philosophical Institute on growing apples and grapes. He also learned the methods by which plants could be artificially pollinated—fertilized by male reproductive cells—by higher-yielding plants to increase their agricultural yield. Higher-yielding plants generate greater amounts of crops per acre than lower-yielding plants. The monastery had botanical and mineralogical collections to help Mendel and other monks in their studies. In the course of his studies, Mendel passed three examinations with honors.

Many members of the monastery were teachers at the Philosophical Institute in Brno or the local high school. These included Abbot Napp, who not only catalogued the monastery's library but also taught biblical studies and the oriental languages. Some of the monks left the monastery after a few years to become professors in universities. Friedrich Knapp, for example, eventually went to Olomouc as a professor of physics. One monk, Anton Keller, had published scientific papers on breeding different varieties of melons. Another, Anton Thaler, had an experimental garden in which he grew rare plants. Mendel was to take over the garden in later years. So when he became a monk, Mendel gained exposure to many of the leading scientific and intellectual currents of his time.

Novices were entrusted to the care of Anton Keller, who was an active member of several agricultural societies. Keller had not only published a scientific article describing alternative traits of six different varieties of melon but also had a special interest in the economic aspects of breeding new varieties of fruit trees and palms. So right from the start, Mendel was in the company of an acknowledged expert on agriculture.

Mendel appreciated the advantages that the monastery and its monks gave him. He wrote that he had achieved the security that is "so beneficial to any kind of study." He worked with the monastery's small botanical and mineralogical collections and was able to spend a lot of time studying natural science, for which he said he had "a special liking, which deepened the more he had the opportunity to become familiar with it."

But the monastery was not completely immune to political influences. In 1848, a revolutionary movement spread across the Austro-Hungarian Empire, demanding such changes as more civil liberties an end to feudal labor. Mendel was not much affected by the revolution, which eventually was crushed, but he did sign a petition demanding more freedom and civil rights for all citizens, and especially for monks, who under the old regime lost all their civil rights when they entered a monastery. The petition said that "in the frenzied call for liberty," no thought had been given to members of religious orders, who had to endure "enforced isolation." It asked that monks be given "free, united, and indivisible citizenship."

Mendel may have signed the petition because of his unhappiness with his duties. Among the tasks he was given when he became a monk was to give spiritual care to the sick people in the local hospital. He did not like the assignment. The main reason was that it did not give him the freedom to study natural science. He sought some way to give up that position and become a teacher, which would allow him to pursue scientific studies. One result of his unhappiness was an illness that confined him to bed for more than a month. It appears that he was again suffering from exhaustion due to the stress he was experiencing. He had to be attended by a nurse from the nearby hospital of the Brothers of Mercy, which cost the monastery considerable money.

What gave Mendel the chance that he wanted was a request made by the school in Znojmo, a nearby town, for someone to teach classics and mathematics in the seventh grade. Until then, the school had taught only the first six grades; it needed teachers because of its expansion. Abbot Napp recommended Mendel, and he took up the position in October 1849, although he did not have the formal university document of approval that was then demanded of all teachers. He was so short of money that he had to ask for an advance on the pocket money that his abbot allowed him. One sign of his poverty was that Mendel could not afford the local laundry and sent his dirty clothes home to be washed.

The letter that Abbot Napp wrote appointing Mendel said that "this collegiate priest lives a very retired life, modest, virtuous, and religious, thoroughly appropriate to his condition," adding that "he is very diligent in the study of the sciences, but he is much less fitted for work as a parish priest, the reason being that he is seized with an unconquerable timidity when he has to visit the sick-bed or to see anyone ill and in pain. Indeed, this infirmity of his made him dangerously ill, and that was why I found it necessary to relieve him of service as a parish priest." Mendel wrote later that he had "followed this call with pleasure" and that "his [Mendel's] sorrowful youth taught him early the serious aspects of life, and taught him also to work. Even while he enjoyed the fruits of a secure economic position [in the

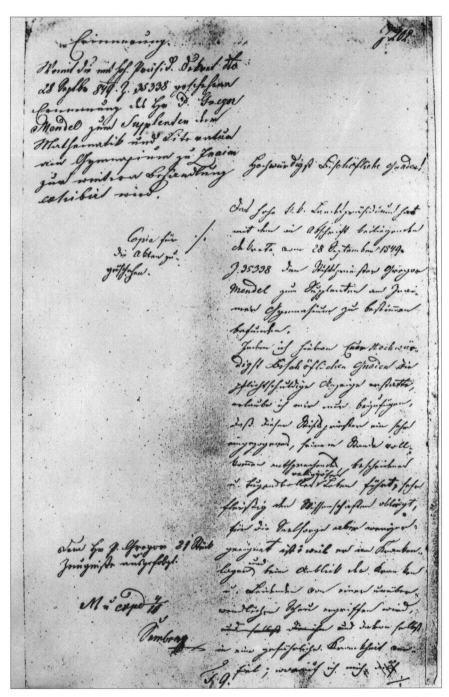

Rough draft of the letter from Abbot Napp to Bishop Schaaffgotsch, in which he states that Mendel is not so fit for church duties and that he is taking up the position of supply teacher of mathematics and literature at the Secondary School at Znojmo.

monastery], the wish remained alive within him to be permitted to earn his living."

The new paychecks that Mendel earned as a teacher helped, as he had hoped. He led a busy life. In school, Mendel taught Latin, Greek, and mathematics, a teaching load of 20 classroom lessons a week. His monthly salary was 360 guilders. A surviving report made by the headmaster of the school said that Mendel quickly learned his teaching material and mastered the basic skills of teaching. The head of the school wrote an assessment that praised Mendel's "vivid and lucid method of teaching," noting especially that Mendel had been able to keep up with the demanding syllabus.

In order to continue as a teacher, Mendel had to take a state-ordered examination. In 1850, when he was 28 years old, Mendel took the examination that was necessary for official approval of his teaching career. He failed. The failure is explainable. Most teachers who took the test had acquired the necessary information that it required over several years of full-time studying in a college or university. Mendel had to do his studying while he was teaching 20 hours a week, overseeing his students, and constantly preparing lessons for his classes. Intelligent as he was, he was not fully prepared for the examination.

For the first part of the examination, Mendel had to write two essays, one on geology and the other on the properties of air and the origin of wind. (The geology question required him to explain "the chief differences between rocks formed by water and those formed by fire, detailing the main varieties of the Neptunian strata in serial number according to their age. . . .") Mendel, with little training in either subject, had to write the essays in eight weeks, while he had his full teaching load.

The essay on wind passed muster, with the professor saying, "The candidate says what he means to say, if not brilliantly, still scientifically, and satisfactorily on the whole." But the essay on geology was rejected, on the grounds that

Mendel had used outdated references and had not discussed the important issues in enough detail. (Mendel did make some points that are of great interest. Writing eight years before Charles Darwin put forth his theory of evolution, Mendel wrote of early Earth, "Plant and animal life developed more and more abundantly; the oldest forms disappeared in part, to make room for new, more perfect ones." He said of Earth that "so long as its fires burn and its atmosphere still moves, the history of creation is not finished.")

In the second stage of the examination process, Mendel went to Vienna for further tests. Again he was under a handicap. He arrived later than the scheduled date, and because it was the middle of August, his examiners were in a hurry to leave on vacation. In the physics part of the examination, Mendel had to write a paper on magnetism, describing how to make a magnet from a steel bar. The two professors who judged the paper said it was satisfactory. For the other part of the exam, Mendel had to write about mammals, giving examples of animals that were useful to mankind. He did not do well on the second essay or on the oral part of the

Mendel attended the University of Vienna from 1851 to 1854.

examination and was told to take the examination again, but not until a year had passed. Mendel returned to Brno with the fear that his career as a teacher was over.

If Mendel had passed the teachers' examination, he probably would have stayed on at the Znojmo *Gymnasium* permanently and his story would have been completely different. Several generations of secondary school children would have gained an excellent teacher. Science, however, might have lost one of its leading discoverers, because Mendel might not have had the time to do his plant research.

To give Mendel another chance to pass the teaching examination, Abbot Napp sent him to the University of Vienna to study natural history. Mendel entered the university in 1851 and stayed almost two years, a period of enormous excitement and progress for him. In his letter of recommendation, Napp wrote, "Father Gregor Mendel has proved unsuitable for work as a parish priest, but has on the other hand shown evidence of exceptional intellectual capacity and remarkable industry in the study of natural sciences, and his praiseworthy knowledge in this field has been recognized by Count Baumgartner. But for the full practical development of his powers in this respect it would seem necessary and desirable to send him to Vienna, where he will have full opportunities for study."

Not much is known about Mendel's private life at the university. He did not have a lot of money and was ten years older than the rest of the students, so he probably did not have much of a social life. While he did his university studies, he also performed his obligations as a priest, saying mass regularly. Just two of the letters he wrote during that time have survived. In one, he asks a friend to help him buy new shirts, since the laundry had lost twelve of his. In the other, he tells his parents that he is in good health and all is going well, that he is studying hard, and that "I hope that time will tell." He also wrote indignantly about an attempt to assassinate the Austrian Emperor.

At the university, Mendel came into contact with some of the leading scientists of the time, including Franz Unger, a known expert in plant physiology and cytology (the study of cells), who was one of Mendel's teachers. Mendel also met Karl Naegeli, a renowned plant expert, with whom Mendel later corresponded for many years. Much of what we know about Mendel comes from the letters he exchanged with Naegeli.

Another meeting that was to prove important over the years was with Christian Doppler, director of the Physical Institute and professor of experimental physics at the university. Today Doppler is noted for his discovery of the Doppler effect, the observed change in the frequency of sound, light, and other waves that occurs as the distance between the wave source and the observer changes rapidly.

Botanist Karl Wilhelm Naegeli studied cell division and osmosis. He and Mendel exchanged scientific papers and notes on experiments.

Then as now, physics was a science in which mathematics played a central role. Mendel's exposure to Doppler and other instructors at the Physical Institute made him familiar with the mathematical analysis of natural events. Among other subjects, he studied the statistical principles of meteorology, and combinatorial analysis, which deals with such subjects as permutations and combinations. Permutations and combinations are different ways in which the numbers of a set can be arranged for their study by a mathematician.

What Mendel learned from Franz Unger was also important for the future. Unger studied and taught about the development of plants from the historical point of view, going back to specimens found in ancient geological formations and following the development of more modern species; he also studied hybrids. His view, the generally accepted view of the time, was that the crossing of two plants to create a hybrid—the F1 generation—produced a uniform set of plants. When the hybrid F1 generation plants were crossed, the resulting plants in the F2 generation were believed to revert to the traits of the original crossed species or varieties. In the reports he wrote about his studies,

Cross of two hybrid round peas: Each parent (F1 generation) contributes one dominant and one recessive allele. The resulting generation (F2) exhibits both dominant and recessive traits.

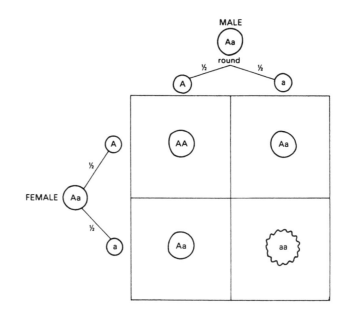

Unger did not state the percentage of F2 plants that resembled each of the two original species. That percentage was not thought to be important, and biologists were not used to working with such mathematical terms.

What Mendel got from Unger was exposure to new methods of experimental research. Unger had been influenced by J. M. Schleiden, who wrote that "every hypothesis and every induction in the science of botany must be rejected if it does not have as its aim the explanation of any process taking place in the plant as a function of the changes which take place in its individual cells"—in modern terms, that studies had to examine the genetic makeup of individual plant cells and the changes that occur in those cells over time. Mendel's later research was done in accordance with Schleiden's rule.

Unger wrote that a plant is "an artificial chemical laboratory, the most ingenious arrangement for the play of physical forces." Unger rejected the idea of constant species, saying that a process of metamorphosis occurred continually. "Who can deny that new combinations arise out of this

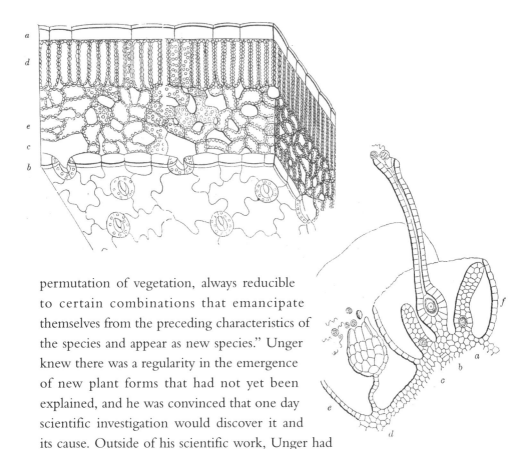

permutation of vegetation, always reducible to certain combinations that emancipate themselves from the preceding characteristics of the species and appear as new species." Unger knew there was a regularity in the emergence of new plant forms that had not yet been explained, and he was convinced that one day scientific investigation would discover it and its cause. Outside of his scientific work, Unger had bold political views and was attacked for what his critics described as agnostic and socialist opinions.

Mendel also came in contact with a book written by a Viennese astronomer, L. L. Littrow, who stressed the importance of the newly discovered theory of probability. Littrow wrote, "All phenomena, even those which seem most dependent on pure chance, exhibit, when they are repeated often enough, a tendency to more and more constant relations, and are subject to some usually very simple law from which, if it is once recognized with sufficient precision, the future conditions of the phenomenon can be predicted." That statement, which said that many phenomena in nature could be explained in mathematical terms, guided the experiments that Mendel was to do with a large number of

Illustrations from Botanical Letters by Franz Unger. Top: cell structure of a leaf. Bottom: fertilization in a plant, including (b) the female part of the plant with egg cell, and (d) the sperm-producing or male part of the organism.

plants, the experiments that led to the laws of genetics.

When Mendel finished his studies in Vienna, he returned to Brno at the end of July 1853. He resumed teaching in May 1854, even though he did not take the examination needed to qualify as a teacher of natural history. A position as a teacher of natural history and physics at a newly opened *Realschule* (high school) was created for him.

He was a good teacher. He taught large classes, between 62 and 109 pupils. He had at least 18 classes a week, sometimes as many as 27, and also was responsible for managing the school's natural science collections. A biographer who spoke to some of Mendel's former pupils decades later found that they all praised him as a conscientious, kind, and just teacher, who was good at what he taught. They gave a physical picture of him: "A man of medium height, broad-shouldered and already a little overweight, with a big head and high forehead, his blue eyes twinkling in the friendliest fashion through his gold-rimmed glasses. Almost always he was dressed, not in a priest's robes, but in the plain clothes worn by members of the Augustinian order who worked as teachers: frock coat, usually rather too big for him; short trousers tucked into top-boots."

His pupils liked him. Later one of them remembered "his cordial tone of voice, . . . his justice and conscientiousness, his gentleness and his smile." Decades later, one of his students recalled him "standing in front of his pupils, looking at them in a most friendly fashion." Another who had been taught by Mendel said, "All his pupils agreed in extolling his method of instruction. . . . There was no need for him to have recourse to terror as a supplement to instruction. His clear and luminous method of exposition, reinforced in case of need by subsequent friendly elucidations, enabled all his hearers to understand what they wanted to understand. He himself delighted so much in his work as a teacher, and was able to present every topic so agreeably and invitingly that we always looked forward to our lessons."

As a teacher, Mendel was considerate and patient. At the end of the school year, he asked the pupils who had been given low grades whether they wanted to be re-examined. Then he would have the pupils make up questions for one another. The students were encouraged to visit Mendel in the monastery garden, where he could give them needed explanations or special tutoring. He had a haphazard way of selecting students to be examined in the classroom. He would pick a number at random out of his notebook, 12 for example, and then say, "Twice 12 is 24, and 24 plus 12 is 36." Then he would examine the student whose number was 36.

In 1855, Mendel applied once more to take the teachers' examination. He took part of it in Brno and part of it in Vienna. When he had to do the written part of the examination in Vienna, he had one of his nervous collapses and became so ill after answering the first question that he could not complete the rest of the test. This second failure did not stop Mendel from being a teacher; he continued at his old position for many years. But it did mean that he earned only half the regular teachers' pay.

In the longer run, Mendel's failure to get a teacher's license was important in one way. It allowed him to continue to study in Vienna and to come in contact with scientists and methods that would prove important in his studies of heredity. Even as he taught, Mendel began the series of experiments with plant breeding that were aimed at answering one of the basic and most important questions in biology: What is inherited and how? The answers that Mendel obtained from his plants became the foundation of a new science.

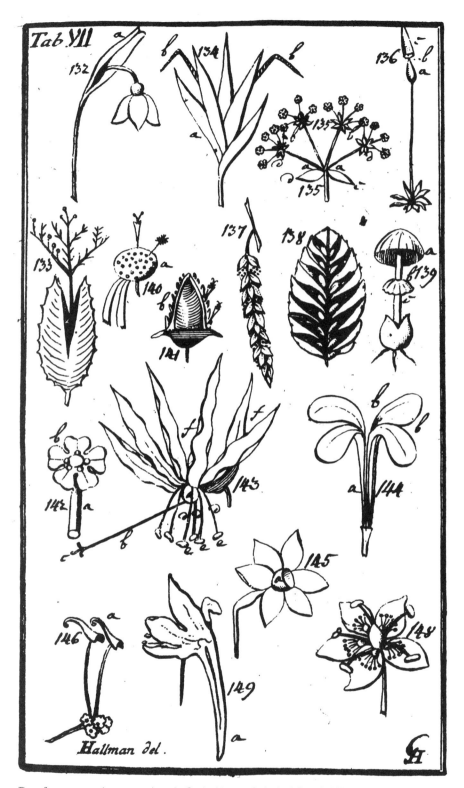

These flower types and parts were drawn by Carolus Linnaeus for his book Botanical Philosophy, published in 1751.

Mendel Begins Plant Experiments

When Mendel returned to Brno from Vienna in 1853, he had already made plans for a research program on heredity. As he wrote later, "The selection of the plant group which is to serve for experiments of this kind must be made with all possible care if it be desired to avoid from the outset every risk of questionable results."

In his research, Mendel used a discovery that had been made not long before: Plants have sex. It had long been assumed that plant flowering and reproduction simply happened. The first and most important step toward reversing that view came when an 18th-century scientist, Carolus Linnaeus, devised a new system of plant species classification that made plant sex the basis of species determination. Linnaeus also described hybrids. (When Mendel told his students about plant reproduction, often using plain street terms, some of the students would titter. "Don't be stupid! These are natural things," Mendel would say.)

Starting in the late 1700s, a German scientist named Joseph Koelreuter conducted a series of experiments showing that plant reproduction required that a grain of pollen, the male element in plant fertilization, must fertilize the plant equivalent of an egg to produce a seed that will grow into an adult plant. Plants can be self-pollinating, Koelreuter showed, but they also can be fertilized by pollen from other plants.

Koelreuter also conducted a long series of experiments in plant hybridization. When he started, only two well-known plant hybrids had been produced by artificial cross-pollination. His first hybrid was sterile; the plants did not produce seeds and the pollen grains were shrunken and sterile. But when he back-crossed these plants with pollen from plants of the previous generation, he did get fertile hybrids.

Over several years, Koelreuter produced the first accurate record of plant hybrids. The first-generation (F1) hybrids, he wrote, had characters that were mostly intermediate between those of the parent plants. The F2 and back-crossed hybrids were all different, with characteristics that resembled those of the parent plants in varying ways. Koelreuter's explanation: The bewildering variety of characteristics was the result of combining plant materials "not intended for each other by the wise Creator"—hardly a scientific explanation. But he did note that in some hybrid generations, the plants had characteristics of the grandmother generation, the grandfather species, and the F1 parents, in the ratio of 1:2:1. He concluded that hybrid species sooner or later revert to the traits of one or the other original species.

Joseph Koelreuter, pioneer in plant hybridization experiments, was the first to recognize the importance of insects and the wind in pollinating flowers.

Decades later, in the mid-19th century, a German botanist, Carl Gaertner, repeated some of Koelreuter's hybrid experiments, and did a large number of his own. The plants that he crossed included peas, tobacco, and corn. He observed that some traits were dominant, appearing in generation after generation, even as others disappeared in some generations and re-emerged later. He could not explain his results in a coherent way; he simply said that "the total nature of the species" determines the direction and form of hybrids.

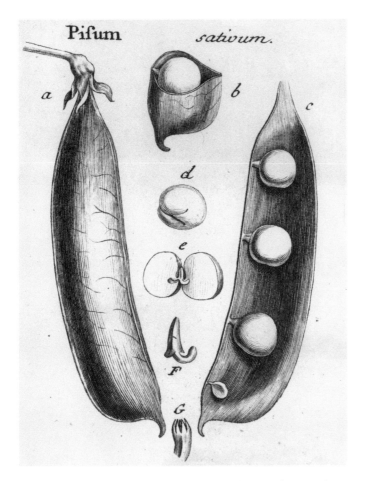

A 1791 drawing by J. Gaertner of the garden pea Pisum sativum, *with which Mendel began his experiments in plant hybridization.*

So when Mendel began his work with peas, he was doing the same sort of work that others had done. The difference— a huge difference—was in the conclusions he drew from his observations.

First he had to select the goal of his research. As he explained later, it was to determine exactly how traits are passed from generation to generation—"a question whose significance for the developmental history of organic forms must not be underestimated."

The plants he chose for his first experiments were varieties of peas belonging to the genus *Pisum*. The reasons, he later explained, were that *Pisum* produces fertile hybrids that can reliably be distinguished from one another, it can easily

This page from Mendel's notebook lists crosses between various kinds of beans. A later geneticist described this sheet as "a hasty sketch of an idea, comparable with the study sketch of a painter."

be protected from cross-pollination, and it can be grown in both gardens and greenhouses. (The monastery had a small garden, and also a greenhouse that Mendel could use.)

We have one firsthand glimpse of Mendel's work with pea plants. A young representative of a large French plant-breeding company named C. W. Eichling visited Mendel's monastery in 1878, following the advice of a noted hybridist, Ernest Benary. Decades later, Eichling wrote that after lunch, Mendel showed him "several beds of green peas in full bearing, which he said he had reshaped in height as well as in type of fruit to serve his establishment to better advantage. I asked him how he did it and he replied, 'It is just a little trick, but there is a long story with it which it would take too long to tell.' Mendel had imported more than 25 varieties of peas, whose peas shelled out readily [could easily be obtained from the shells] but did not yield very well because some of them were bush types. As I recall it, he said that he crossed these with his tall local sugar-pod types, which were used at the monastery. I told Mendel that I had promised to make a report to Benary regarding these experiments, but Mendel changed the subject and asked me to inspect his hothouses."

Mendel used two unusual approaches to his experiments. First, he tested the plants for two years to be sure that the traits he was studying were constant, recurring from generation to generation. The botanists who had done previous hybrid experiments did not conduct such tests of constancy. Second, Mendel was careful to distinguish between constant hybrids, whose traits persisted unchanged for generations, and variable hybrids, in which parental traits might change in some generations. Again, previous botanical studies had not made that distinction.

Mendel studied at least seven traits of different strains of *Pisum,* including the position of its flowers on the stem, differences in stem lengths, the color of the unripe pod, the shape of the ripe seed, and the color of the seed coat. It was his study of seed shape that has become most famous.

In what has become a classic experiment, Mendel crossed a variety of *Pisum* that had round seeds with a variety that had wrinkled seeds. The first generation (F1) of plants all had round seeds. The next year, Mendel planted the round seeds and looked at the seeds of the resulting F2 generation plants. There were 5,474 round seeds and 1,850 wrinkled seeds—a ratio of almost exactly 3 to 1, he recorded. When Mendel planted the F2 generation seeds, he found that all the plants growing from the wrinkled seeds had wrinkled seeds. Of those growing from the round seeds, one-third had round seeds only, while the other two-thirds produced both round and wrinkled seeds, again in the 3:1 ratio. Mendel did six other experiments to look at the inheritance of other traits in the pea plants and got remarkably similar results, with the same three-to-one mathematical ratios for inherited traits.

So far, Mendel's results did not differ greatly from those achieved by Koelreuter and Gaertner. What was different was the mathematical analysis that Mendel used on the results, the conclusions he drew from that analysis, and the language he used to describe his conclusions—all of which were to become foundation stones of the new science of genetics.

The round-seed trait that the F1 generation plants had, the trait that persisted in every generation, Mendel called "dominating" (a term later changed to "dominant"). The wrinkled-seed trait of some of the *Pisum* plants, the trait that disappeared in the F1 generation and reappeared in following generations, Mendel called "recessive," a term that is still used.

As an explanation of his results, Mendel proposed that each plant had two elements that determined seed shape. Any plant that had either one or two elements for the dominant trait displayed that trait—in the case of the most-noted *Pisum* experiment, round seeds. To display the recessive trait (for *Pisum,* wrinkled seeds) a plant had to have two recessive elements. Mendel used a capital letter A to describe the dominant trait and a small letter a to describe the recessive trait. So a plant with two dominant elements would be AA, one with a dominant and a recessive element would be Aa, and one with two recessive elements would be aa. Geneticists still use that notation.

Mendel did a number of other experiments, looking at other traits of the pea plant. All the results were consistent with those of the seed study. For example, in a study of stem length, long and short, the dominant trait (long stem) occurred in 787 of the plants, or 73.96 percent, the recessive strain in 277 plants, a ratio of 2.84 to 1; In a study of seed coat color, the ratio of dominant to recessive was 3.15 to 1—in both cases close enough to the ideal 3:1 ratio to support Mendel's conclusions.

One of the conclusions that Mendel drew from the experiments was that each of the different traits of the parents and offspring is determined by specific elements—today we use the word "genes"—a specific element for each trait. This statement has become known as Mendel's first law, or the Principle of Segregation. One simplified example would be that there is one element, or gene, that determines a person's hair color and another, completely different, element, or gene, that determines eye color. The genes for eye color and for hair color are passed from generation to generation.

Another of Mendel's conclusions was that these elements, or genes, are inherited separately, without affecting

This diagram illustrates the cross of two varieties of Pisum, *those with round and wrinkled (angular) seeds. The hybrids are all round, but when crossed together, round and wrinkled peas segregate in the ratio 3:1.*

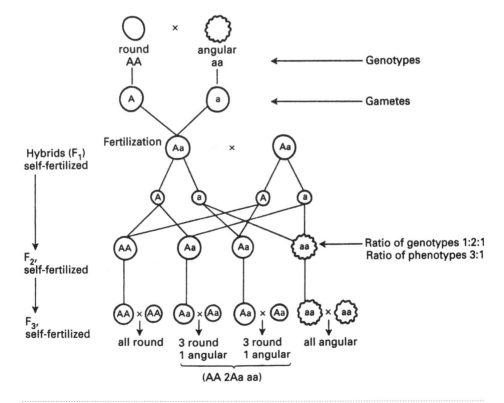

each other. This has become known as Mendel's second law, or the Law of Independent Assortment of Traits. As Mendel expressed it, "the behavior of each pair of differing traits in a hybrid association is independent of all other differences in the two parental plants." One example would be that the element, or gene, for hair color and the element, or gene, for eye color are inherited separately. This law later was modified, when Thomas Hunt Morgan, a 20th-century American biologist, discovered the phenomenon called linkage: Linkage can occur when two or more genes are situated very close to each other on the same chromosome, the cellular body that contains genetic material; genes that are close together may often be inherited together.

A third of Mendel's conclusions was that each inherited characteristic, such as eye color or hair color, is determined by the interaction of two elements, or genes for that trait, one from each parent. In the characteristics that he studied, Mendel found that one element always predominated over the other. This theory became known as the Principle of Dominance.

To summarize Mendel's findings in simple form and using today's language:

1. Each inherited trait is governed by a gene. Genes for a specific trait can exist in different forms, which today are called alleles. For example, one allele of the gene for hair color can make a person blond, while another can make a person dark-haired. In other words, alleles are slightly different varieties of the same gene.

2. Each individual, plant or animal, has two sets of genes, one set inherited from each parent.

3. The genes are usually transmitted unaltered from generation to generation. The traits of each generation are produced by a reshuffling of the gene combinations of the past generation.

4. Gene alleles can be dominant or recessive. An individual who inherits two dominant alleles or a single dominant

allele for a trait will display that dominant trait. To display a recessive trait, an individual must inherit two recessive alleles for that trait.

(Mendel's work did not touch on the mutations, or changes, that can occur in genes as they are passed from generation to generation. Mutations can have many effects, good and bad. They are responsible for genetic diseases, but they also are the source of changes that are the basis of evolution. Many other scientists, most notably Charles Darwin, have dealt with the effects of mutations.)

Mendel published a paper describing his results and conclusions under the title *"Experiments in Plant Hybridization"* in the *Proceedings of the Natural Science Society* of Brno. He ordered 40 reprints, which he sent to a number of scientists and institutions. No one paid much attention. A few of the reprints have been tracked down. In most cases, they were obviously unread, because the pages were uncut. The scientific world simply ignored Mendel's findings and explanations. A major reason was that Mendel was not a well-known scientist in a leading university or scientific institution. Another was that scientists were simply not ready to receive such advanced findings.

Mendel's essential conclusion was that "the ratio of 3:1 in which the distribution of the dominating and recessive traits takes place in the first generation therefore resolves itself into the ratio of 2:1:1 in all experiments if one differentiates between the meaning of the dominating trait as a hybrid and as a parental trait." In other words, a plant that displayed the dominant trait—round seeds in the case of the *Pisum* experiments—might have two dominant genes (AA), or one dominant gene and one recessive gene (Aa); for every AA plant, there were two Aa plants. He was explaining the difference between the appearance of the trait, which now is called the "phenotype," and the underlying genetic basis for that appearance, which now is called the "genotype."

text continues on page 53

MENDEL AND DARWIN

The two great figures in the 19th-century study of living things were Gregor Mendel and Charles Darwin. Like the rest of the world, Darwin was completely unaware of Mendel and his work. But Mendel left ample evidence that he knew of Darwin's work and made a thorough study of it.

Darwin's epoch-making book, *On the Origin of Species,* was published in 1859, just as Mendel was completing his experiments with *Pisum*. Darwin's theory of evolution—the survival of the fittest through gradual changes in individuals through the generations—could potentially be regarded as hostile to Mendelian genetics, because some people could say that individual animals and plants changed in response to the environment, and that these changes were passed on to future generations.

Charles Darwin in 1852.

Such a view was promulgated by Jean Lamarck, the 19th-century French scientist who said that acquired characteristics were inheritable. But there was a major difference between Lamarck and Darwin: Lamarck spoke of individuals, while Darwin dealt with populations. Darwin did not say that an individual animal or plant changed in response to environmental conditions. Instead, he said that in any large population there were bound to be slight differences in characteristics—the length of the neck of the giraffe is one good example—and those differences led to evolution.

In the case of the giraffe, Darwin wrote, individuals with slightly longer necks were better able to get leaves off trees, and so were better fed and healthier and were more likely to have offspring with longer necks. Those offspring, in turn, were likely to have offspring with even longer necks, and so on until giraffe necks reached an optimum length for feeding from trees. Darwin never tried to describe the mechanism by which characteristics such as neck length were passed to future generations. In one of his books, he expressed an inability to understand how parental traits could appear in hybrid offspring—the very thing that Mendel's work with plants explained.

Mendel read Darwin's books and left marginal comments on them. In his copy of *On the Origin of Species,* Mendel marked the statements that species are not immutable and that it seems clear that organic beings must be exposed during several generations to new conditions to cause any great amount of variation. And in a later Darwin book, *Variation in Animals and Plants under Domestication,* Mendel expressed strong disagreement with Darwin's statement about several spermatozoa or pollen-grains being necessary for fertilization. Mendel had already found that a single pollen grain sufficed.

In general, however, Mendel's comments and notes did not indicate disagreement with Darwin's basic theory of evolution. And over the longer run, Mendel's work did provide an explanation of how traits were transmitted to future generations, and how they could slowly change over the years and decades.

One tantalizing question is whether Mendel and Darwin ever met. There was one opportunity, when Mendel joined a traveling party that visited England. A meeting seems doubtful, however, since Mendel was a very modest man, while Darwin already had become internationally famous. Last but not least, Mendel could not speak English.

The first page of the manuscript of Mendel's Experiments in Plant Hybridization, which was published in 1865.

text continued from page 49

The word "phenotype" derives from the Greek word *phaino*, "to display," while the word genotype derives from "gene."

In his next series of experiments, Mendel investigated whether the laws of inheritance that he had deduced for one pair of traits would hold good for two unrelated traits. In these experiments, he crossed purebred pea varieties whose seeds differed in both shape (round or wrinkled) and color (yellow or green). Mendel labeled the dominant and recessive forms of the two traits A, a, and B, b. Mendel obtained 556 seeds from 15 hybrid plants:

> 315 were round and yellow
> 101 were wrinkled and yellow
> 108 were round and green
> 32 were wrinkled and green.

In the paper he wrote, Mendel had equations that denoted the combination of the traits in simplified form as: A + 2Aa + a, and B + 2Bb +b. When he planted the 556 seeds, he got 529 plants whose characteristics can be expressed in the form of a table.

	AA	**Aa**	**aa**	**Total**
BB	38	60	28	126
Bb	65	138	68	271
bb	35	67	30	132
Total	138	265	126	529

Mendel placed these hybrids in three different groups. The first included the forms AB, Ab, aB, and ab, which possess constant traits that do not change in succeeding generations. There were about 33 plants in each of the four groups. The second group consisted of plants that were constant for one trait and hybrid for another: Abb, aBb, AaB, Aab. There were about 65 plants in each of these groups. The third group of plants were hybrid for both traits: AaBb. There were 138 plants in this group.

The basic principle, Mendel wrote, was that "constant traits occurring in different forms of a plant kindred can, by means of repeated fertilization, enter into all the associations possible within the rules of combination." Mendel expressed the numbers of the four groups in the ratio 4:2:1. Years later, when the 20th century began, geneticists used the ratio 9:3:3:1 for four different trait combinations in the off-spring of hybrids.

Mendel briefly mentioned "several more experiments carried out with a small number of experimental plants" in which he looked at the inheritance of more than two separate traits. He said that he had actually obtained all of the combinations possible with seven different traits of *Pisum*. There were 128 such traits, a number that can be expressed as 2 to the 7th power. His mathematical conclusion: "If n denotes the number of characteristic differences in the two parental plants, then 3 to the nth power is the number of terms in combination series, 4 to the nth power the number of individuals that belong to the series, and 2 to the nth power the number of combinations that remain constant." Small wonder that the nonmathematical plant experts to whom the paper was sent did not grasp its significance.

Some biologists had proposed the idea that one plant species could be transformed into another by artificial fertilization. One biologist, Carl Gaertner, reached the conclusion that since plant hybrids tended to revert to their parental forms, there was no way to create new, stable hybrids. Mendel differed with that view, based on his new techniques of studying plant hybrids. Using the example of the crossing of plants with three different traits, Mendel said crossing those plants would produce eight kinds of germinal cells:

ABC, ABc, AbC, abC, Abc, aBc, abC, abc.

When a hybrid plant is fertilized with pollen seeds abc, Mendel said, the following cells would be produced:

AaBbCc + AaBbc + AabCc + aBbCc + Aabc + aBbc + Aabc + aBbc + abCc + abc.

The experimental garden where Mendel began to study pea plants is this fenced area on the monastery grounds.

Since one in every group of plants would have the genes abc, Mendel said, it would be possible for any single trait to obtain a transformation of that trait even in the first generation. But he added, "the smaller the number of experimental plants and the larger the number of differing traits in the two parental species, the longer an experiment of this kind will last, and, furthermore, a delay of one or even two generations could easily occur with these same species."

Mendel himself grew a large number of plants for his *Pisum* experiments. He noted that "For two generations all experiments were conducted with a fairly large number of plants. Starting with the third generation, it became necessary to limit the numbers because of a lack of space, so that, in each of the seven experiments, only a sample of those plants of the second generation could be observed further. The observations were extended over four to six generations."

One biologist has estimated that Mendel grew as many as 24,000 plants in his experiments with *Pisum*. Mendel also did experiments with other species. For example, he crossed plants of the *Phaseolus* bean genus that had long stems, and yellow pods with plants that had short stems and green pods. He reported that the green pod and long stems were the dominant traits, adding that the results of his crosses "also proceeds according to the law of the simple combination of traits, exactly as in *Pisum*." Another set of *Phaseolus* bean plant crossings were "only partly successful," Mendel said, in part because he was crossing different species of the plant and the resulting hybrids had reduced fertility. For plant shape, the results fit the *Pisum* laws, but the results for plant color did not; Mendel got a wide range of colors, from purple to white.

Mendel did many more plant experiments with a number of different species. The largest number of experiments was done with many varieties of *Hieracium,* a plant that was abundant in the region. More than 22 of Mendel's experiments with varieties of *Hieracium* have been recorded. He wrote and published a paper describing some of those experiments, but it went unnoticed, even many years later after his work with *Pisum* had become famous.

Although he did publish some papers in scientific journals, Mendel reported most of his observations on plants other than *Pisum* only in his letters to a German scientist, Karl Naegeli. A British scientist, A. H. Sturtevant, said that those letters gave a picture of a man who was very actively experimenting, aware of the importance of his discovery, and testing and extending it on a wide variety of forms. Sturtevant added that Mendel's work might not have been ignored so completely if he had published this extra evidence.

All the while Mendel did his plant experiments, he was carrying his load as a teacher and as an active member of the monastery. Mendel wanted to continue his plant studies indefinitely, but in 1868, something happened that changed his scientific efforts and his life forever.

Upon being elected as abbot, Mendel wrote, "From the very modest position of teacher of experimental physics I thus find myself moved into a sphere in which much appears strange to me, and it will take some time and effort before I feel at home in it."

Mendel Becomes the Abbot

The event that changed Mendel's life was the death of Abbot Napp, the head of the Brno monastery, in March 1868. In a letter to Naegeli, Mendel described "a completely unexpected turn in my affairs. On 30 March my unworthy self was elected lifelong head by the chapter of the monastery to which I belong." He quickly added that the election "shall not prevent me from continuing the hybridization experiments of which I have become so fond; I even hope to be able to devote more time and attention to them, once I have become familiar with my new position." Because he would no longer be working as a schoolteacher, he hoped to have more time to spend on his experiments.

Mendel wanted to be abbot. At that time, he was paying for the schooling of one of the sons of his younger sister, and he faced the prospect of financing the education of her two other sons. He clearly needed the extra money that the post would bring him. He could also stop teaching, which would give him more time for his plant research. Before the vote, he wrote to his younger sister's husband saying, "should the choice fall on me, which I scarcely dare hope, then you will receive a telegram next Monday. If you do not receive one, someone else has been elected."

The choice of the new abbot was made by a vote of members of the monastery. After two rounds of voting, there was no winner. Mendel won on the third round of voting, with 12 votes, when the other major contender stepped aside. Mendel became abbot on March 30, 1868, when he was 46 years old. The telegram to his sister was sent.

It was a position that was of more than religious importance; there were ethnic, economic, and political considerations as well. The monastery community had equal numbers of monks who were of German origin and those who were Czech. Tension between the two ethnic communities in Brno had been increasing for years. The police paid enough attention to the monastery election to write a memo stating that the election of any one of three specific Czech monks would be undesirable. Mendel, of Germanic origin, won because the Czechs swung their support to him. For reasons of politeness, Mendel himself voted for one of the Czech monks, Martin Klacel, who clearly had no chance to win. In the end, Klacel voted for Mendel and persuaded some of his supporters to do the same, believing that Mendel's liberal views would make him a better abbot than any of the other candidates.

The signature of Abbot Mendel, in German and Czech.

As abbot, Mendel immediately had to tackle some complex economic issues. A major fight that affected the monastery was brewing. Mendel's monastery had never been taxed before. Suddenly the Austro-Hungarian government was demanding that the Brno monastery pay 34,000 guilders into a state-run religious fund that would help pay the stipends of parish priests. Mendel wrote a 12-page letter saying that the monastery could not pay such a sum, because it was already deep in debt and the size of the community was only a quarter of what it had been years before. He noted that a major reconstruction of the church and other buildings, costing 30,000 guilders, was needed. He also cited public service as a reason why the government should get no money from the monks: The monastery had provided teachers for several academic institutes, and two monks who worked in the local hospital had died from infections they contracted there. Mendel did offer to pay 2,000 guilders in taxes, but the government would not accept so little. The argument dragged on for years and was not settled until after Mendel's death.

A Polish stamp from 1939 with a portrait of Mendel, part of a series portraying eminent German scientists.

There were also political changes to consider. In 1867, the Hapsburg Empire had become the Austro-Hungarian constitutional monarchy. It was a democracy of sorts. The new government began to make changes. One of them was to transfer the responsibility for schools from the Catholic Church to the state. Church leaders protested, but Abbot Mendel supported the change at first because he believed in state support of schools, a stand that did not please Church leaders. Mendel drew back from his stand.

He did arouse controversy by his political activities. The first political parties in Austria-Hungary started when the new government structure was created. Officially the government granted equal rights to the predominant German and Hungarian ethnic groups. (The rights of other ethnic groups such as the Czechs were not mentioned in the law granting those rights.) Political parties were organized along ethnic lines. The party that represented the interests of ethnic Germans was the German Constitutional

Party, also called the Liberal Party. It was opposed by the Conservative National Party, in which the Catholic Church was active.

Mendel was expected to support the Conservative National Party, so there was astonishment and alarm when he came out in favor of the Liberal Party in the provincial diet, or legislature. Church leaders and Czech monks in his monastery became openly hostile to him when he signed a Liberal Party petition opposing the election of a Conservative Party member. Mendel continued to express his political views, but he became a bit quieter about them. And when he was offered a chance to become a Liberal Party candidate for the parliament, he politely turned it down. But he continued to express support for the Liberal Party's policy on the troubling ethnic issue of equal rights for ethnic Germans and ethnic Czechs. Mendel's activities eventually won him a government honor, the Order of Franz Josef, for "outstanding political work and meritorious teaching."

After 1867, Mendel was much more cautious about his political activities and statements. He concentrated much more on his scientific interests, which were many and varied. One of them was meteorology—the weather—where he gained wide recognition as one of the best meteorologists in his region of the country. Mendel began making meteorological observations at the monastery in 1857, assisted by a local physician, Philip Olexik. Mendel monitored wind direction and force, using a flag on the tower of a nearby castle to indicate the direction of the wind and the speed of smoke from chimneys for the force. He also kept records of rainfall and of ozone levels. Ozone is a harmful form of oxygen; Mendel was interested in it because of its potential for damaging crops. The ozone concentration was monitored on a ten-degree scale, from zero to 100, according to the color changes recorded by paper that Mendel treated with liquid nitrous iodine and a starch solution.

Mendel published a paper on his weather observations in 1862 in the *Austria-Hungary Natural Science Society Proceedings*. His data were shown in a large-format graph. The graph included the daily values of observations in the morning, at noon, and in the evening; five-day averages of wind direction, wind force, and cloud cover; and five-day rainfall averages. The most remarkable feature of the paper was a comparison of the 15-year average with the yearly observations. Mendel used statistical principles well before other meteorologists did—the same kind of statistical analysis that he used in his plant studies. People later asked whether he had learned to use statistical analysis of his plant studies from his weather work. The answer seems to be that he learned the statistical method when he studied physics, and applied those principles to both his weather and plant studies.

A compass Mendel used to make meteorological observations. A member of the Vienna Meteorological Society, he was considered the greatest authority on the subject in Brno and Moravia.

The Natural Science Society was so impressed by the paper that it had 500 extra copies printed for distribution. When a network of meteorological observation points was established in the region that year, Mendel's paper, with both the timing of the observations and the statistical analysis he used, was the basis for the publication of the observations. One measure of Mendel's interest in weather studies was that in his obituary his membership in the Vienna Meteorological Society was the first mention after his name. His membership in the Natural Science Society, where he gave lectures on his work with peas and other plant hybrids, was not even mentioned.

Mendel made full use of his meteorological experience when a tornado struck Brno on October 13, 1870. The tornado swept past his monastery at two in the afternoon, and Mendel observed it from an open window. He wrote detailed observations of the storm, first reporting them at a meeting of the Brno Natural Science Society and then publishing a 10-page report in the society's journal the following year.

The first part of his report was a physical description of the storm as a "hellish symphony, accompanied by the crash of window panes and slates, which in some cases were flung through the shattered windows to the other side of the room." And he also estimated the storm's size, direction of rotation, and speed as it traveled through Brno. Mendel's published explanation of the origin and course of the tornado, elaborated with mathematical and geometrical reasoning, has become famous. He ended on a light note: "This brings to an end the discussion of our dangerous guest. But we must admit that, however we might have tried, we have got no further than an airy hypothesis."

Although Mendel's last publication of his weather studies was in 1870, he continued to make his weather observations, but he was too busy with other things to keep up a regular schedule of publications.

Mendel also spent years monitoring water-table levels, apparently responding to an article that connected fluctuations in those levels with epidemics of various diseases. Starting in 1865, Mendel monitored the level in the monastery well, something he did until 1881. Mendel did not reach any conclusions, but the effort illustrates his drive to accumulate data on natural occurrences and to detect patterns in them. His data were published years later, after Mendel had become famous for his genetic work.

Mendel was also an eager amateur astronomer. The link between weather studies and astronomy was sunspots, the dark spots that appear on the face of the sun; the idea of a connection between sunspots and the weather had recently emerged. In 1882, from January to the end of November, Mendel carefully recorded his observations of sunspots. Only a few fragments of his observations have survived, and it is not known how far he carried his astronomical work. But his astronomical telescope has survived and is on display in Brno; it is displayed simply because it was Mendel's.

Most of Mendel's research concerned agriculture, and it included work on bees. Beekeepers then were actively trying to increase honey yields by crossing different species of bees. An Apicultural (Beekeeping) Association was organized in Brno in 1854, primarily through the efforts of Abbot Napp, Mendel's predecessor, and a national congress on beekeeping was held in Brno in 1865, again under Napp's leadership.

Mendel's father had kept bees in his garden, so Mendel was familiar with the subject. After the 1865 meeting ended, Mendel had built in the monastery's garden a beehouse that contained a number of beehives; it still stands. He gave every hive in the house a number and kept records of the installation of queen bees, swarms, bee traits, and other factors. He wrote that "it is important for every beekeeper to carry out experiments, since this is the only way to achieve successful results."

Mendel cross-bred bees from Cyprus, Egypt, and even South America. One of his goals was to improve honey yields, but he also wanted data to confirm the theory of heredity that came from his work with peas. He devised an ingenious cage with screens and doors that enabled him to control matings, and worked on various arrangements to control the matings in the best way. He achieved results that were remarkably similar to those reported by 20th-century bee researchers.

One of Mendel's more important bee studies was done with Anton Tomaschek, a natural history teacher at the Brno Technological Institute. They worked with a tropical bee species called *Trigona lineata,* for which Mendel devised a new type of special house. Papers describing the bees' honeycombs, reproduction, cross-breeding, and honey manufacture were published in zoological journals. As one journal editor wrote, "We must acknowledge the

The bee house in the garden of Mendel's monastery may be considered the first center for bee research in central Europe.

experiments with the acclimatization of *Trigona* bees in Europe by Tomaschek and Father Mendel as the most successful for fruitful science."

One of Mendel's reasons for doing bee research was to confirm his theory of heredity by crossing different races of honey bees. To get such crosses, he built another special cage that would allow a queen bee of one race of bees to mate with a drone from another race. A beekeeper from Hungary, Franz Kuehne, visited Mendel in 1879 and wrote a report on that visit. He described the mating cage as "very ingenious," but noted that Mendel's mating experiment had failed; the queen bee died without even coming close to the drones in the cage. Mendel explained the failure by saying that "the drones were taken from the alighting boards of various hives and knew the pleasant feeling of free flight. They were not therefore willing to undertake such an important act as mating in the confines of an enclosure."

Kuehne kept in touch with Mendel after the visit, and sent a letter asking whether later experiments had succeeded. Mendel said they had not. "Last year the fault lay in the drones, this year in the queen." The queen, Mendel said, "remained quite indifferent to her passionate lovers and repeatedly tried to escape from the cage." This time it was the queen who had known free flight and was not willing to mate in an enclosure, Mendel explained.

He continued with his bee-mating work, designing new enclosures and trying new combinations of queens and drones. Eventually he did succeed in cross-breeding, and he became an acknowledged expert on many aspects of bee-breeding and bee-raising.

For this work, Mendel was made an honorary member of the national beekeeping association, and was elected vice-chairman in 1871. He was offered the position of chairman in 1874, but turned it down. Not long afterward, he stopped most of his work with beekeeping so that he could concentrate on his work with plants.

Mendel did a great deal of work on breeding flowers such as the fuchsia, working with local plant breeders. He did a lot of research with another plant breeder, Johann Twrdy. Twrdy's daughter later wrote that Mendel often met her father in connection with the work, and that they were linked by an endeavor to use artificial crossing and artificial selection of plants to obtain far-reaching results. Mendel was a frequent guest in the Twrdy garden, she wrote.

Twrdy had been a gardener for an aristocratic estate, and later became one of Europe's most noted flower breeders. He was fond of naming his new varieties of flowers after famous individuals, many of them scientists such as Galileo and Alexander von Humboldt. Twrdy showed his appreciation of Mendel's contribution by naming a new variety of fuchsia after him in 1882. The "Prelate Mendel" variety was described as being very large, "pale-blue shading into violet, luxuriant, with regular structure, the sepals light, very beautiful, and blooming early." It does not seem to have survived to our time.

But Mendel's primary interest as a plant breeder was in fruit trees and vines. He grew more than 500 seedlings of pear, apple, and apricot trees in the monastery garden. In 1883, Mendel exhibited new varieties of apple and pear trees at a meeting of the Gardeners' Association in Hietzing, on the outskirts of Vienna, and was awarded a prize and the association's medal. The new varieties that Mendel created were grown in many gardens well into the 20th century.

In 1870, Mendel was elected a member of the central committee of the Moravian and Silesian Agricultural Society. He was re-elected regularly, and in 1872, he became deputy to the society's director. The next year, he was officially made vice-chairman. Mendel was offered the post of chairman in 1882, but he turned it down on grounds of ill health. He continued to attend meetings of the society until the illness that led to his death.

Mendel was also a good citizen. Fires occurred frequently in his old home town of Hyncice, making inhabitants poorer and often homeless. Abbot Mendel not only proposed the establishment of a local fire brigade but also offered to contribute 1,500 guilders of the monastery's funds to buy fire-fighting equipment. By June of 1882, his proposition had been accepted, and pumping equipment had arrived in Hyncice. The grateful villagers made Mendel an honorary member of the fire brigade, which pleased him greatly.

Mendel's feelings about his priestly duties were expressed in a surviving draft he made for an Easter sermon. Mendel took special note of the way that Christ appeared to Mary Magdalen when he rose after his crucifixion: as a gardener. He wrote that "the gardener plants seed or seedlings in prepared soil. The soil must exert a physical and chemical influence so that the seed of the plant can grow. Yet this is not sufficient. The warmth and light of the sun must be added, together with rain, in order that growth may result." Mendel used this image from the world of nature to illustrate how "the germ of supernatural life, sanctifying grace, is put into the soul of man." So even as a priest, Mendel referred to his work with plants.

Mendel visited Hyncice for the last time in 1873, when he performed the wedding ceremony for his nephew, Alois Sturm. When his nieces and nephews visited Brno, they stayed in lodging opposite the monastery, so they could be in close contact with their uncle. He liked to play chess with them, and took delight in giving them difficult chess problems to solve.

And so Abbot Mendel lived a useful, productive life, sometimes even being noticed by the greater world outside his monastery for some of his scientific efforts. But the world paid little or no attention to his most important research, the genetic studies that were to found a new science and established its basic principles. And the political and ethnic controversies in which he was involved began to have an effect on his health. He became a heavy smoker, often smoking 20 cigars a day. One of his nephews, Alois Schindler, noted that Mendel's pulse rate was often as high as 120; a normal pulse rate is well under 100.

In his last years, Abbot Mendel lived a largely solitary life. He looked forward to visits by his nephews, who stopped at the monastery when they passed through Brno going to and from Vienna. In a letter he wrote in 1883, Mendel asked his nephew to bring him grafts from the old fruit trees in his parents' garden, so that he could grow them at the monastery. It was one of the last letters that he wrote.

Abbot Gregor Mendel's official emblem. In the upper left-hand corner of the crest is a fuchsia bloom, which he chose as his personal symbol. In the lower right-hand corner, the Alpha and Omega, first and last letters of the Greek alphabet, symbolize the Christian belief in God's eternity and Infinitude.

Mendel's Last Years

Mendel's final years were made difficult by a running con-
flict he had with the new government in Vienna, which in
1875 passed a law requiring monasteries to pay taxes on
their property—7,330 guilders a year for the Brno
monastery. Mendel was the only head of a monastery in the
country who refused to accept the law, a stand that he
maintained until he died. Others argued with him about the
issue. Community members pointed out that the law had
been passed by the liberal political party that Mendel supported. Lawyers told him that he could never win his fight.
Mendel persisted and became known as "the stubborn
prelate." In a plea he made to the government in 1877,
Mendel said that because of the fight, he had "gone grey
and grown old before his time." People began to regard him
as something of a crackpot. "He is full of suspicion and sees
himself surrounded by nothing but enemies, traitors, and
intriguers," one lawyer wrote of him.

Nevertheless, Mendel persisted in his refusal until he
died. His last protest against the law imposing taxes on the
monastery was written in May 1883. In June, the local government asked the Bishop of Brno whether he could do

anything to end the controversy, hinting that the amount of the tax could be reduced considerably. At that time, Mendel was so ill that the economic affairs of the monastery were being handled by another monk, Ambrose Poye. When Poye received a note rejecting Mendel's protest, he did not show it to Mendel. Instead, he sent it back to the government, saying that the abbot was seriously ill, enclosing a letter from Mendel's doctor that said Mendel had "conditions in which a perfect repose is essential and all emotional disturbances must be avoided." Poye sent a protest to Vienna, complaining about the amount of tax that was being required. The tax was paid by Mendel's successor, but eventually the monastery was relieved of payment for the decade that began in 1880.

Some of Mendel's work for the Brno monastery can still be seen. When the tornado damaged the roof of the monastery's chapter hall in 1870, Abbot Mendel not only had it repaired but also had the ceiling decorated with paintings proposed by him. In the middle of the ceiling was a portrait of Saint Augustine and his mother, Saint Monica. Paintings at the four corners reflected Mendel's scientific interests. One showed fruit-tree grafting. Another showed meteorological instruments, a globe, and maps. A third showed an old and a new beehive, and the fourth was a portrait of Saint Isidore, the patron saint of agriculture.

Two of the ceiling frescoes Mendel commissioned for the Brno monastery. This page: Saint Isidore, patron saint of agriculture. Next page: an old and new beehive.

When the hall was renovated decades later, the paintings were removed, but one of the monks had the foresight to take photographs of them. Eventually, when Mendel's fame had spread, the paintings were re-created. Visitors can see them today, and can also see the original paintings Mendel ordered for the monastery's library, which have survived untouched.

And Abbot Mendel was a good family man.

He paid for the studies of his sister Theresa's three sons at the Brno *Gymnasium*. He helped put the oldest son, Johann, through the Brno Technical University and gave financial aid for the two younger sons when they studied medicine in Vienna. One of his last letters was written to his nephew Alois Schindler, a physician and professor of internal medicine, asking him to come to Brno to talk over an important professional matter. That matter was the treatment of the kidney disease from which Mendel suffered. Alois told him that not much could be done. Alois said that his uncle awaited his death unemotionally, as something that had to happen. But one thing Mendel did insist on was a postmortem examination to determine the nature of the illness that caused his death.

All of these details were made public only decades later, when Mendel's greatness as a scientist was established. Suddenly, half-forgotten memories of him became important.

Abbot Mendel had fallen ill in 1883, as his kidney disease which he had suffered from for years became more acute. He went to a spa in the city of Roznov that summer to recuperate, but the visit did him little good. By autumn, he was unable to go out into the monastery garden. On December 20, he wrote a letter to a former pupil saying that he was no longer able to make his meteorological observations, concluding, "Since we are unlikely to meet again in this world, let me take this opportunity of wishing you farewell, and of invoking upon your head all the blessings of the meteorological deities." Mendel's last letter was written to his nephew Alois Schindler, asking him to come to Brno. Alois did make the trip and observed that Mendel was awaiting death stoically, with little change in different

Dr. Alois Schindler (left), Mendel's nephew, wrote a biography of his uncle in 1902. This was the basis for many other publications in different countries, as other scientists became interested in Mendel's work.

health risks. Mendel's medical condition grew worse on January 4, 1884, and he died two days later, in the early morning hours.

The cause of Mendel's death was listed as chronic inflammation of the kidneys and abnormal overgrowth of the heart. An account of his death has recently come to light, written by a native of Brno: "My mother often talked about Mendel and his last hours, for the duty of looking after Mendel was assigned to her and a nun. She washed the bandages which were bound around the abbot's feet and which needed changing many times a day. He suffered from loss of water, chiefly from the feet. It was a protracted and painful illness, but he rarely complained. He spent most of the time sitting on the sofa, going to bed only when he felt sleepy. The bandages were almost dry on the day of his death. My mother said to him, 'Your Grace, today you have already no water.' 'Yes, it is already better,' answered the abbot. When the nun was making the bed, she found him sitting on the sofa dead."

His funeral took place on January 9. It was attended by government officials, clergy of the Catholic Church and other religions, representatives of the many organizations in which he had been involved, and a number of the poor people who Mendel had always tried to help. After the ceremony, the attendees followed the coffin to the Central Cemetery, where Mendel's coffin was placed in the monastery tomb. It still can be seen there, in the northeastern corner of the enclosure.

The local newspaper paid a tribute to Mendel: "His death deprives the poor of a benefactor, and mankind at large of a man of the noblest character, one who was a warm friend, a promoter of the natural sciences, and an exemplary priest."

Clemens Janetschek, one of the monks in the monastery, wrote a poem after Mendel's death, describing him as:

> Gentle, free-handed, kindly to one and all,
> Both brother and father to us brethren was he.
> Flowers he loved, and as a defender of the law he held
>   out against injustice.
> Whereby at length worn out he died from a wound of
>   the heart.

The longest obituary, published by the local agricultural society, noted that in 1859, Mendel had grown "exquisite vegetables," and that everything he did "took on a practical importance." It added almost in passing that his experiments with hybrids "opened a new era." The obituary said that "Father Gregor Mendel did not satisfy himself with lifeless words, but took an active hand in the agricultural affairs of

Moravia at every opportunity, and always and in everything paid great attention to them."

The poem, and the various obituaries, seem today to have missed the point. Mendel's really important scientific work went unnoticed at his death. As far as the world was concerned, Abbot Mendel was a holy man who did some interesting, but minor, scientific research. We have noted that one monk recorded Mendel's words about scientific work: "My scientific work brought me much satisfaction, and I am sure it will soon be recognized by the whole world."

If there are doubts about that quotation, it is because it is almost too good to be true. His day was yet to come. The obituaries that described Mendel's deeds, including his scientific work, did not make any mention of Mendel's findings about inheritance, the findings that would make any remembrance of him noteworthy years later, when the world slowly became aware of his long-ignored work. The rediscovery of that work after Mendel's death makes a fascinating story.

6

Mendel Rediscovered

Mendel's work was rediscovered not just once but three times, by three different researchers, in the course of a few years some three decades after Mendel's death.

Why did it take so long? In 1903, Gregor Niessl, a biologist in Brno, wrote that Mendel's findings simply did not fit in with "the spirit of the age" during his lifetime. "His work was well known but ignored in the prejudice raised by the divergent and mutually exclusive views current at the time," Niessl said. "From personal contact with Mendel of many years' standing I knew that he did not succumb to disappointment as a result of the fact that his botanical publications did not meet with immediate success at the time when for the explanation of the origin of new forms of plants the principles of the then generally acknowledged hypotheses of Darwin were almost exclusively decisive."

Another plant breeder who spoke often with Mendel about his work recorded one simple statement that Mendel made: "My time will come." But the process of recognition may have been held back by Mendel himself. Throughout his later life, Mendel kept up a continuous correspondence with a well-known German scientist, Karl Naegeli.

Eenige gevallen van Klemdraai bij de meekrap.

Hugo de Vries, Opera.

Fa. P. W. M. Trap impr.

Botanical drawings by Hugo de Vries, published in 1920, show his interest in how interior structures relate to the exterior appearance of plant species.

Mendel's letters to Naegeli included detailed accounts of his experiments with plant species other than *Pisum*. Each of those letters, with very little change, could have been published as a scientific paper. For reasons that are not known, Mendel made no effort to publish them so the wider scientific community in Europe could know what he was doing. In one of his early letters to Naegeli, Mendel not only described an experiment but also included a packet of seeds, with the suggestion that Naegeli repeat the experiment. Naegeli did not take up the challenge, and Mendel never mentioned the proposal again.

There was one case in which another scientist, Heinrich Hoffman, did include a mention of Mendel's work on a number of plant species in a scientific paper in 1869—a mention that was important even though it made a mistake in describing Mendel's rules about the heredity of hybrid plants. That mention might have spurred Mendel to publish results of his later experiments, to correct Hoffman's mistake, but again he did not. His theory had to wait until 1900, 16 years after his death, to be recognized.

The long process of rediscovering Mendel's work started with a Dutch biologist, Hugo de Vries, in the late 1880s. De Vries collected examples of plant monstrosities and, in 1885, began breeding experiments, much like the ones Mendel had done, with an unusual form of thistle, later adding experiments with a flower, the evening primrose.

These experiments led de Vries to reject the idea, then held by many scientists, that the changes caused by the effects of the environment during an organism's life could be passed on to the next generation. Instead, he said that units within the living cells carried the information of heredity.

De Vries called the theory of heredity that he derived from his experiments "intracellular pangenesis." *Intracellular* means inside the cell, and *pangenesis* was a term invented by de Vries. He said that the hereditary units, which he called pangenes, were responsible for changes in species.

Hugo de Vries, in a pen-and-ink drawing by Robert Kaster. De Vries signed it with the following words, in French:
"Every phenomenon of life has its external causes as well as its internal causes."

"An altered numerical relation of pangenes already present, and the formation of new kinds of pangenes must be the two chief factors of variability," de Vries wrote in 1889.

The existing belief that an individual member of a species was the basic unit of heredity was wrong, de Vries said. Instead, the basic units were the pangenes. And by 1889, de Vries's work on the genetics of specifically crossed plants showed the same sort of percentage of varieties as Mendel had found years earlier. For example, de Vries found that crossing *Lychnis vespertina* with *Lychnis vespertina glabra* produced 392 plants with the hairy characteristic of the first species and 144 with the smooth characteristics of the second species—close to the 3 to 1 ratio that Mendel already had described.

In 1900, a friend sent de Vries a paper, with the note that, "I know that you are studying hybrids, so perhaps the enclosed reprint of the year 1865 by a certain Mendel which I happen to possess is still of some interest to you." De Vries later wrote that he had learned of Mendel's paper "only after I had completed the majority of my experiments and had deduced the principles given in the text." Doubts have been raised about that claim. There is evidence that de Vries knew about Mendel's work fairly early, that he borrowed heavily from Mendel, and that this knowledge played a large role in shaping de Vries's scientific reports.

According to one scientist who has studied de Vries and his work, seeing a reprint of the *Pisum* paper in 1900 "must have disturbed him greatly. . . after studying the paper he was prepared to absorb the idea of numerical segregation ratios. He therefore quickly published selected data from his own previous experiments, and only then referred to a segregation ration of 3:1, using Mendel's terms dominant and recessive."

In one of his papers, published in 1900, de Vries cited Mendel's work specifically to help explain the results of his plant breeding experiments. After describing his own experiments, de Vries wrote, "From these and other numerous experiments I draw the conclusion that the law of the segregation of hybrids as discovered by Mendel for peas finds very general application in the plant kingdom, and that it has a basic significance for the study of the units of which the species carriers are composed."

A second scientist given credit for rediscovering Mendel's work was Karl Correns, a noted German botanist. Correns was working on the inheritance of characteristics of maize (corn) and peas. Correns said he worked out the same 3 to 1 ratio for dominant and recessive traits for the studies he was doing at some time in 1899, but he was uncertain about the exact date. What is known is that Correns received a copy of de Vries's paper, which mentioned Mendel's work, in 1900, and immediately published his own paper entitled "G. Mendel's Law Concerning the Behavior of Progeny of Variable Hybrids." Correns also said that "Mendel's paper is among the best that have ever been written about hybrids. . . ." Nevertheless, Correns said he had discovered the 3:1 ratio before hearing of Mendel's work. He wrote later that "it came to me like a 'flash' as I lay toward morning awake in bed, and let the results run through my head. Even as little do I know the date upon which I read Mendel's memoirs for the first time; it was at all events a few weeks later." In generalizing Mendel's theory, Correns was the first person after Mendel to state not only the 3:1 ratio for single traits but also the 9:3:3:1 ratio for multiple traits.

The third scientist linked with the rediscovery of Mendel's rules is Erich Tschermak von Seysenegg, who was working in Vienna. Tschermak began breeding experiments with peas in 1898 on an estate near Vienna. A paper by Tschermak that was published in an Austrian scientific journal in 1900 reported that his cross-breeding of pea plants had produced 1,854 yellow-seeded and 660 green-seeded

text continues on page 86

DID MENDEL CHEAT?

The charge that Mendel had fiddled with his results to make his published numbers fit his theory was first made by a distinguished British scientist, Sir Ronald Fisher. Fisher first expressed his doubts when he was in college. In 1911, Fisher wrote about Mendel's statistics in the *Pisum* paper, "It may have been just luck; or it may have been that the worthy German abbot, in his ignorance of probable error, unconsciously placed doubtful plants on the side, which favored his hypothesis." Fisher's accusation went unnoticed for many years, but a full-scale scientific debate started several

Sir Ronald Fisher, in a 1943 photograph.

decades after Fisher published a magazine article detailing his charge in 1936.

Fisher made a detailed analysis of the experiments in which Mendel crossed first-generation plants to look for the occurrence of dominant and recessive forms. After a detailed statistical study, Fisher concluded that there was only one chance in 30,000 that Mendel would have arrived at his published numbers by chance.

Some scientists supported Fisher. An American scientist, R. S. Root-Bernstein wrote that "Mendel's results are statistically unlikely." They could be used only as clues to his method of classification, not to support his findings, Root-Bernstein said.

But most geneticists rallied around Mendel. One American geneticist, Francis Weiling, who published no fewer than 15 papers analyzing Mendel's results, concluded that Fisher had used the wrong mathematical methods in his study. If the proper method was used, Weiling said, Mendel's results and his honesty were untouched by criticism. Nevertheless, a pupil of Fisher, A. W. F. Edwards, wrote in the 1980s that all the bad-mouthing of Fisher's doubts about Mendel had not altered the truth of his findings. Edwards added that Mendel's results were too good to be true—the numbers were closer to his expectations than chance alone would dictate.

The results are striking. In one experiment, Mendel counted 5,474 round seeds and 1,850 wrinkled seeds, a ratio of 2.96 to 1. In another experiment, Mendel counted 6,002 yellow seeds and 2,001 green seeds, a ratio of 3.01 to 1. In real life, Fisher and his supporters said, those numbers were just too good to be the results of chance.

Politics and ideology came into the argument. In the Soviet Union and Soviet-controlled countries, some biologists attacked Mendel as a way of supporting the theories of Trofim Lysenko, the Soviet pseudoscientist who said that Communism could produce a better breed of human beings in a generation or two, in spite of anything that Darwin or Mendel had done. Those criticisms vanished when the Soviet Union went out of business.

Today, hardly anyone would argue with the conclusion reached by the 20th-century American geneticist Sewall Wright, after a prolonged study: "There was no deliberate effort at falsification."

Fisher himself, while he never withdrew his charges, did ultimately pay his own form of tribute to the abbot of Brno: "The facts available in 1900 were at least sufficient to establish Mendel's contribution as one of the greatest experimental advances in the history of biology," Fisher wrote.

plants, a ratio of 2.8 to 1, and 884 smooth-seeded and 288 wrinkle-seeded plants, a ratio of 3.1 to 1. Tschermak mentioned Mendel's findings in his paper, although there still are arguments about how much of Mendel's findings he rediscovered and how much he simply stole.

But the rediscovery of Mendel's principles was not as simple and as direct as it might seem. In 1901, for example, de Vries wrote to another scientist, "I am now writing the second part of my book which treats of crossing, and it becomes more and more clear to me that Mendelism is an exception to the general rules of crossing. It is in no way *the* rule! It seems to hold good only in derivative cases, such as real variety characters."

As for Correns, he would later write that Mendel's rules "can only be applied to a certain number of cases. . . . That all pairs in all hybrids follow it is quite out of the question."

Tschermak was equally cautious. He later wrote about "limitations and complications" that made the Mendelian scheme lose "its general validity." Tschermak thus had only a limited role as a rediscoverer of Mendel.

Indeed, later analysis challenged the work of all three of Mendel's discoverers. An analysis in 1900 showed that none of the three had gotten as far as the idea of pairs of separate traits that are governed by elements, or genes, in cells and are transmitted to offspring in specific mathematical relationships, most notably the famous 3 to 1. Studies in the 1980s showed that de Vries, Correns, and Tschermak had each accepted only part of Mendel's explanation at first, and had gradually adopted his full explanation and mathematical relationships as they continued their work. Even more than 30 years after his death, Mendel was still ahead of the leading scientists studying genetics.

The most recent interpretation of Mendel's work is that the "rediscoverers" revised their methods after reading Mendel's paper and above all interpreted the results they got by taking Mendel's methods into account. Mendel's observations and his methods of analysis "were new and not easily understood or connectable to the usual patterns of thought about hybridism," one later researcher has written.

In 1910, a British scientist, D. J. Scourfield, summed up the later findings about the three men's work and discovery of Mendel's report: "We can imagine their astonishment as they read that old paper, to find that it actually contained the clue for the puzzle they had themselves been struggling with in the course of their work. They lost no time in making known their discovery, and thus was inaugurated what, from the point of view of the study of heredity, may justly be termed the Mendelian era."

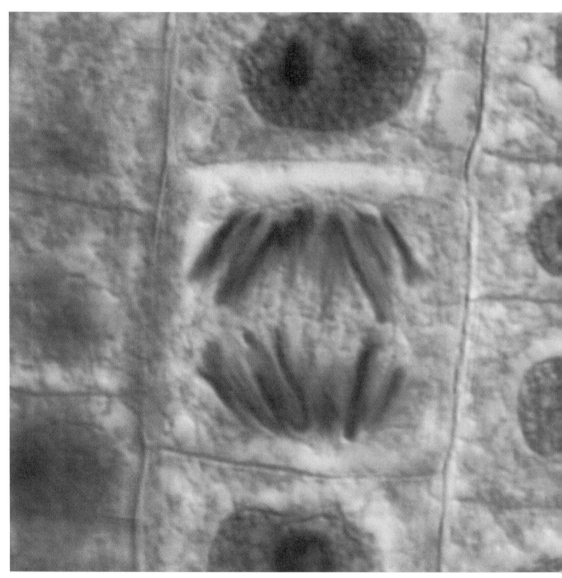

A microscopic photograph showing cell division in plants. In the center cell, the genetic material pulls away to opposite ends of the cell before a wall forms between the two parts, creating two new cells.

Mendel's Legacy

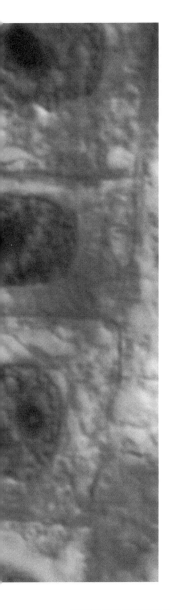

The first international congress on genetics was held in London in 1906. Indeed, it was at that congress that the field got its name. A British botanist, William Bateson, said that the new ideas on plant breeding and hybridization had given birth to a new science, and he said that it should be called genetics, a word he derived from "genesis." Bateson said the name for the new science "sufficiently indicates that our labors are devoted to the elucidation of the phenomena of heredity and variation."

The first description of a human genetic disease and its inheritance had already been made. In 1902, a British doctor, Archibald Garrod, reported his observations of the disease called alkaptonuria, in which the patient's urine turns black on exposure to air. Garrod had traced the inheritance of the disease through several generations in several families, and wrote that it was inherited as a "Mendelian recessive" (a term that Mendel did not coin)—the first demonstration of Mendelian transmission of a characteristic in humans. Garrod went on to describe the exact genetic mechanism of alkaptonuria—the blockage of one specific step in a metabolic pathway, a set of chemical changes that carries out a

Sir Archibald Garrod extended Mendel's theories to explain the heredity of diseases in humans.

basic functions of the body. He called the condition an "inborn error of metabolism," a name that still is used. Garrod identified several other inborn errors of metabolism, including cystinuria (which causes excess formation of bladder stones) and albinism, the lack of skin color. By 1990, more than 5,000 genes whose mutations are involved in metabolic diseases had been identified, and the work of discovery goes on.

One question had to be answered early on: What exactly were Mendel's "elements." Part of the answer came in 1879 from a German biologist, Walther Flemming, who discovered processes in living cells by using dyes that were absorbed by some parts of the cell but not by others. In particular, Flemming studied the nucleus of the cell, the small, membrane-enclosed portion often found toward the center.

Flemming found that the dyes that he used were absorbed by a material in the nucleus that he named chromatin, from the Greek word for color. By using his dyes in cells at different stages of their life cycles, Flemming found himself observing an unusual sequence of events.

The chromatin would first gather itself into threadlike bodies. Then the membrane surrounding the nucleus would dissolve. A new object, which Flemming called the aster because it had a starlike shape, then appeared. The aster divided in two, and the two parts went to the opposite ends of the cell. There were strands radiating from the two parts of the aster, and they attached themselves to the threads of chromatin and slowly pulled the chromatin apart. These threads, which Flemming called chromosomes (again, from the Greek word for color), were soon at opposite ends of the cell. Then the cell divided, forming a wall between the two parts, and new nuclei formed in each new cell around the chromosomes. At the end of the process, there were two cells, each with a full complement of chromosomes.

No one knew what to make of Flemming's observations until 1902, when Walter S. Sutton, an American scientist, pointed out that Flemming's chromosomes and Mendel's factors, or genes, had a lot in common. Both were transmitted from generation to generation. Studies of the sex cells, sperm and egg, showed that each had a nucleus containing a half set of chromosomes. When the sperm and egg united, they formed a cell with one nucleus and two sets of chromosomes. That fit with Mendel's observation that each individual, plant or animal, inherited one set of genes from each parent.

There was one major difficulty in saying that the chromosomes were genes: There weren't enough chromosomes—only eight (in four pairs) in fruit flies, only 46 (in 23 pairs) in humans. There were obviously a lot more genes than that in fruit flies, humans, or any organism.

Thomas Hunt Morgan won the Nobel Prize for his discoveries relating to the existence of genes for specific traits located at specific sites on chromosomes.

An American, Thomas Hunt Morgan, helped to solve that problem. Morgan worked with the fruit fly, *Drosophila*. To start, all his fruit flies had red eyes. But one day, a fly with white eyes appeared in one of the cages. Morgan bred this white-eyed fly, a male, with a red-eyed female. Soon there were many red-eyed descendants, but none with white eyes—an indication that the gene for white eyes was recessive. Following Mendel's lead, Morgan bred the red-eyed descendants with each other. He got a big surprise.

The surprise was not the ratio of red-eyed flies to white-eyed flies. That was 3 to 1, expected from the Mendelian rules. The surprise was that all the females had red eyes, while all the white-eyed flies were male. This was something that Mendel's rules did not explain.

Morgan found the answer. He proposed that the gene for red eyes and the gene that determined female sex were on the same chromosome. Looking at the chromosomes under the microscope, Morgan found that only three of the four pairs were evenly matched in size. In the fourth pair, those two chromosomes were identical in females, but one of the two was noticeably smaller in males. A small chromosome and a full-sized one produced a male, while two full-sized chromosomes produced a female. Today it is known that what is true of the fruit fly is true of all species in which the male and female sex organs differ. Because of their shape, the full-sized sex chromosome has come to be called the X chromosome, while the smaller one, found only in males, is called the Y chromosome.

The next question to be asked: What are the chromosomes made of? Most biologists believed that they had to be proteins, because these molecules perform so many of the basic functions of the body. (A protein is a chain made up of subunits called amino acids). Proof that chromosomes were not proteins came from a team headed by Oswald Avery at Columbia University in New York.

Avery worked with pneumococcus, the bacterium that causes pneumonia. Pneumococcus comes in two forms, smooth (S) and rough (R). The R-form is harmless; the S-form causes a deadly infection. In 1928, a British scientist, Frederick Griffith, reported that a strain of the R-form could transform a killed strain of the S-form into a virulent form. Avery and his colleagues set out to find the transforming factor. They grew pneumococci in the lab and treated the bacteria to remove all their sugars and proteins, because they wanted to look at a different kind of molecule that had been discovered decades earlier by Johann Miescher, a Swiss scientist working in Germany.

Looking at the cell nucleus, Miescher had isolated a new compound, rich in phosphorus and with large molecules, that he called nuclein It consisted of protein and another ingredient, which was called nucleic acid. By the beginning of the 20th century, the three constituents of nucleic acid had been determined. One of them is a sugar called ribose, which has a ring of five carbon atoms (table sugar, sucrose, has two rings with 12 carbon atoms). The second constituent is a phosphate, which is a phosphorus atom surrounded by four oxygen atoms.

The third constituent is an organic compound that acts as a base. By the turn of the century, five such bases, differing slightly in composition, had been described: adenine, guanine, cytosine, thymine, and uracil. A unit of a nucleic acid consists of a sugar, a phosphate, and a base.

It soon became apparent that there are two different kinds of nucleic acid. One of them, with a full ribose unit, is called ribonucleic acid, or RNA. The other has one less oxygen atom in its ribose and is called deoxyribonucleic acid, or DNA. DNA differs from RNA because its bases include thymine but not uracil. Avery and his colleagues established that the transforming principle, which controls the genetics of an organism, is DNA. He had to be cautious about publishing his results, because many biologists were opposed to the DNA theory. But eventually it was established and accepted.

How does DNA transmit genetic information? The answer was established by a number of scientists, the most noteworthy of whom were Francis Crick, a Briton, and James Watson, an American. They discovered the basic structure of DNA—two long chains that wind around each other in a double helix. Each adenine in one chain is matched by a thymine in the other, and each guanine is matched by a cytosine. DNA transmits genetic information by coding for proteins, the molecules that do most of the work of the cell. A protein is made up of individual units called amino acids. Three-nucleotide units of DNA code for the 20 different amino acids that are found in human cells. The genetic code has been worked out, and biologists now know the three-base codes for all of the amino acids. Many enterprises have emerged from that knowledge. Perhaps the most noteworthy is the Human Genome Project, whose goal is to

Watson and Crick's original demonstration model of the double helix showing the distinctive coiling of the two strands of a DNA molecule.

determine the complete makeup of all the chromosomes in the human body. When that project is completed—probably in the early 21st century—the work begun by Mendel more than 150 years ago will have reached a climax.

Francis Crick (left) and James Watson during a walk. In the distance is King's College Chapel at Oxford.

A climax, but not a conclusion. The mysteries of inheritance are endless, and work on discovering answers and applying them to plants, animals, and humans will go on indefinitely. Mendel's achievements provided the basis for that work.

The Human Genome Project is the ultimate fulfillment of the work that Gregor Mendel began. Its goal is to determine the complete sequence of all the bases in all the human chromosomes, and to find the location of all the genes in those chromosomes.

The idea of the genome project originated in the mid–1980s through initiatives taken by two scientists, Robert Sinsheimer at the University of California at Santa Cruz and Charles DeLisi, director of the Office of Health and Environment of the U.S. federal Department of Energy. Saying that "for the first time in all time, a living creature understands its origin and can undertake to design its future," Sinsheimer proposed a major Santa Cruz project on the human genome. The Department of Energy, whose roots went back to the Manhattan Project that developed the atomic bomb, had long sponsored research on the biological effects of radiation, especially genetic mutations. It maintained GenBank, a major database where the sequences of DNA that make up genes and chromosomes are stored. DeLisi proposed to expand that program to obtain the base-sequence information for an entire human genome.

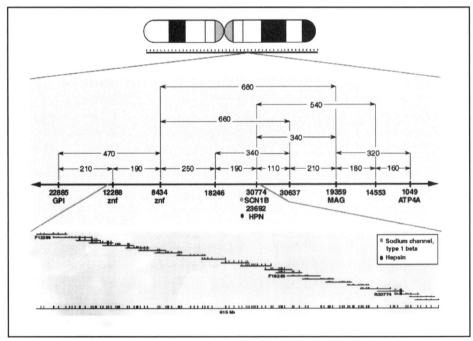

A metric physical map for human chromosome 19, one of the many ways scientists diagram the sequence of DNA bases.

In 1985, Sinsheimer held a meeting at Santa Cruz on a human genome project; in 1986, DeLisi held a workshop on the same subject at Los Alamos. Both their projects were based on the newly developed technology of recombinant DNA, by which a fragment of DNA is snipped out of one genome and spliced into another. The snipping is done by proteins called restriction enzymes, which cut DNA at the site where specific base pairs occur in the DNA chain. Recombinant DNA can be used to isolate single genes and determine their function. Another new technology developed at the California Institute of Technology in the 1980s automated the process of DNA base sequencing.

Restriction enzymes can be used to create markers consisting of DNA fragments from different individuals, because those fragments of the same chromosome differ in length from individual to individual. Restriction fragment length polymorphisms—RFLPs, or riflips—create a framework of genetic markers that allow the mapping of any gene. By the mid-1980s, when Sinsheimer and DeLisi made their proposals, more than 1,500 human genes had been mapped.

After DeLisi proposed a five-year genome project, genome research centers were established at three Energy Department National Laboratories in 1987. The National Institutes of Health established a program in the same year and opened an Office for Human Genome Research in 1988. James Watson, one of the discoverers of DNA structure, was named director. By 1991, the genome project was inaugurated as a formal federal program. In addition to their individual efforts, the Energy Department and the NIH funded some new projects jointly.

In Europe, meanwhile, an international body named the Human Genome Organization, or HUGO, was established in 1988, with help from America's Howard Hughes Medical Institute. Individual genome projects already were being undertaken by most of the major European countries.

Today, with international cooperation and coordination a reality, the genome project is moving along steadily. Sequence data is being added continually to GenBank at Los Alamos and a database at the European Molecular Biology Laboratory. Completion of the project is expected sometime in the early 21st century. That completion will not end the work started by Gregor Mendel, but will give it a new dimension that he surely would have appreciated.

1822
Mendel is born

1840
Mendel graduates from Opava *Gymnasium*

1843
Mendel graduates from Olomouc Philosophical Institute

1843
Mendel enters Augustinian monastery of St. Thomas in Brno

1848
Mendel signs a petition asking for more civil rights for monks

1851
Mendel enters the University of Vienna to study natural history

1853
Mendel returns to Brno to teach

1853
Mendel begins research on plant heredity, publishes paper in the *Proceedings of the Natural Science Society* of Brno

1862
Mendel publishes paper on weather observations in the *Austria-Hungary Natural Science Society Proceedings*

1868
Abbot Napp dies and Mendel is elected the new abbot of the monastery at Brno

1870
Mendel is elected to the Central Committee of the Moravian and Silesian Agricultural Society

1884
Mendel dies

1900
Mendel's genetics paper is discovered by Hugo de Vries and Karl Correns

1902
Walther Flemming makes the first observations of chromosomes

1902
Walter Sutton identifies chromosomes as gene carriers

1900s
Various scientists describe DNA and RNA as carriers of genetic information

1953
James Watson and Francis Crick discover the structural features of deoxyribonucleic acid (DNA)

Mendel's Life and Work

Corcos, A. F., and F.V. Monaghan. *Gregor Mendel's Experiments in Plant Hybrids: A Guided Study.* New Brunswick, N.J.: Rutgers University Press, 1993.

George, W. *Mendel and Heredity.* London: Priori Press, 1975.

Iltis, Hugo. *Life of Mendel,* trans. Eden and Cedar Paul. New York: W.W. Norton, 1932.

Klare, Roger. *Gregor Mendel: Father of Genetics.* Springfield, N.J.: Enslow Publishers, 1997.

Orel, Vítezslav. *Gregor Mendel: The First Geneticist.* Translated by Stephen Finn. Oxford: Oxford University Press, 1996.

Stern, C., and E. R. Sherwood. *The Origin of Genetics: A Mendel Sourcebook.* San Francisco: W. H. Freeman, 1966.

Genetics and Heredity

Arnold, Caroline. *Genetics, From Mendel to Gene Splicing.* Danbury, Conn.: Franklin Watts, 1986.

Aronson, Billy. *They Came From DNA (Mysteries of Science).* New York: W. H. Freeman, 1993.

Ayala, F. J. *Genetic Variation and Evolution.* Burlington, N.C.: Carolina Biological Supply Company Publications, 1983.

Bornstein, Sandy, and Jerry Bornstein. *New Frontiers in Genetics.* Parsippany, N.J.: Silver Burdett Press, 1984.

Bowler, Peter J. *The Mendelian Revolution: The Emergence of Hereditarian Concepts in Modern Science and Society.* Baltimore: Johns Hopkins University Press, 1989.

Crick, Francis. *What Mad Pursuit.* New York: Basic Books, 1988.

Darwin, Charles. *On the Origin of the Species.* Edited by J. W. Burrow. New York: Viking, 1982.

Edie, Maitland A., and Donald C. Johanson. *Blueprints.* New York: Little, Brown, 1989.

Edelson, Edward. *Birth Defects.* New York: Chelsea House, 1992.

Edelson, Edward. *Francis Crick & James Watson and the Building Blocks of Life.* New York: Oxford University Press, 1998.

Edelson, Edward. *Genetics and Heredity.* New York: Chelsea House, 1990.

Frankel, Edward. *DNA: The Ladder of Life.* New York: McGraw-Hill, 1979.

Hood, Leroy, and Daniel J. Kevles. *The Code of Codes.* Cambridge, Mass.: Harvard University Press, 1992.

Joravsky, David. *The Lysenko Affair.* Cambridge, Mass: Harvard University Press, 1970.

Judson, Horace Freeland. *The Eighth Day of Creation.* New York: Simon & Schuster, 1979.

Mayr, Ernst. *The Growth of Biological Thought.* Cambridge, Mass.: Harvard University Press, 1982.

National Research Council. *Mapping and Sequencing the Human Genome.* Washington, D.C.: National Academy Press, 1988.

Nyhan, William L., and Edward Edelson. *The Heredity Factor.* New York: Grosset & Dunlap, 1976.

Olby, Robert C. *The Path to the Double Helix.* Seattle: University of Washington, 1974.

Pomerantz, Charlotte. *Why You Look Like You Whereas I Tend To Look Like Me.* Reading, Mass: Addison Wesley Longman, 1986.

Stefoff, Rebecca. *Charles Darwin and the Evolution Revolution.* New York: Oxford University Press, 1996.

Watson, James D. *The Double Helix.* New York: Simon & Schuster, 1968.

Wilcox, Frank. *DNA: The Thread of Life.* Minneapolis: Lerner, 1988.

INDEX

Edward Edelson is a freelance science writer in New York City. Among the 19 books on science that he has written are two college chemistry textbooks and several young adult books, including *Francis Crick & James Watson and the Building Blocks of Life*. He was the science editor for the *New York Daily News* from 1971 to 1991 and an editor and writer for *Family Health* magazine from 1969 to 1971. He served as president of the National Association of Science Writers from 1979 to 1980 and has received numerous honors from groups such as the American Dental Association, the American Medical Association, the American Institute of Physics, and the American Cancer Society. He holds a B.S. in journalism from New York University and attended the Columbia School of Journalism Advanced Science Writing Program.

Owen Gingerich is Professor of Astronomy and of the History of Science at the Harvard-Smithsonian Center for Astrophysics in Cambridge, Massachusetts. The author of more than 400 articles and reviews, he has also written *The Great Copernicus Chase and Other Adventures in Astronomical History* and *The Eye of Heaven: Ptolomy, Copernicus, Kepler.*